Great Book of Funny Quotes

Great Book of Funny Quotes

· · · · · · · · · ·

Witty Words for Every Day of the Year

▲▲▲

Eileen Mason

Illustrated by Myron Miller

 Sterling Publishing Co., Inc. New York

10 9 8 7 6 5 4 3 2 1

Paperback edition published in 1993 by
Sterling Publishing Company, Inc.
387 Park Avenue South, New York, N.Y. 10016
Originally published in hardcover as *Witty Words*
© 1993 by the Groma Group
Distributed in Canada by Sterling Publishing
% Canadian Manda Group, P.O. Box 920, Station U
Toronto, Ontario, Canada M8Z 5P9
Distributed in Great Britain and Europe by Cassell PLC
Villiers House, 41/47 Strand, London WC2N 5JE, England
Distributed in Australia by Capricorn Link Ltd.
P.O. Box 665, Lane Cove, NSW 2066
Manufactured in the United States of America

Sterling ISBN 0-8069-8605-0

Preface

If, like me, you sometimes can't decide whether you need a vacation, vodka, or Valium, this book is for you.

Humor helps us to get attention, to break up tense situations, and to keep our views of ourselves and the world in balance. Research has even established scientifically that humor (along with other positive emotions) keeps us healthy and helps us to get healthy when we're not, thus proving, in yet another way, what I have long believed: Life is a laughing matter.

This book consists for the most part of quotations chosen for their humorous and witty observations about life. The sources span careers, continents, and centuries: you'll hear from painters, poets, princes, and others, from many countries, and from ancient to modern times—perhaps an indication that the human condition hasn't changed as much as we sometimes think, at that it isn't really so different in different parts of the world. The book also includes well-known and not-so-well-known holidays, as well as some amusing facts, both historical and contemporary.

The book is organized around the calendar, with an index of people quoted and celebrated, a subject index, and a holiday index.

If you are preparing a speech, article, broadcast, newsletter, or other oral or written communication, you can search for material in the three indexes, by the subject you seek, the holiday's name, or the name of the person you wish to quote. The book is thus a practical reference tool for wordsmiths of all types.

It is also a book for simple enjoyment. Place a copy in the waiting room of your office. Plan a celebration of one of the not-so-well-known holidays. Insert a witty quote in a letter. Make a shirt, poster, or plaque for a co-worker, family member, or friend. Design a special-occasion greeting for someone who deserves it.

The items in the book came from various sources, including the fertile imaginations of friends and acquaintances. My thanks go to the thousands who helped provide the material for this book.

—*Eileen Mason*

:⋰⋱: *Mumblings about the "Author"* :⋰⋱:

A lover of words, Eileen Mason began reading at the age of four, and read five books last year—all of them about gambling. She is widely known for her ability to carry on lively conversations—especially by herself.

Sometimes called "Our Lady of Tangents," she has been a secretary (one of her former bosses had a nervous breakdown), production controller, salesman, importer and wholesaler, business consultant, negotiator, advertising/marketing agency, minister, publisher, counselor, and brainstormer. (She also performs brain surgery, but only telepathically.)

Eileen Mason has an M.B.A. in finance, and attended law school for three days. A strong supporter of life-long education, she enjoyed a brief career in university teaching, but had to quit because it interfered with Monday night football. She hates going to libraries, and plans to start a university ("Semper Frivolous").

She abhors shopping and frequently leaves home without her credit cards. Some of the honors she has received are for "World's Greatest Nag," "Most Trips to the Bathroom," and "Southern California's Most Proficient Laundress" (the last from a previous life). She has been certified "Wacko" by a local psychologist and by her husband.

Among her latest endeavors are a grass-roots movement to stamp out home cooking ("It's out of date and deadly on the fingernails"); working for G.O.T.C.H.A.A. (Group Organized To Commence and Hasten the Annihilation of Acronyms); establishing treatment centers for exercise addicts; finding funding for The Funny Foundation ("Bringing Humor to Life"); and a campaign for the U.S. Presidency—her campaign slogan is reportedly "Anyone without a sense of humor will die laughing."

Contents

Blame Someone Else Day

Blame Someone Else Day The first Friday the 13th of the year
"The man who can smile when things go wrong has thought of
someone he can blame it on."—*Arthur Bloch, American writer
(birth date not available)*

January

National Soup Month

National Hobby Month
National Soup Month
"Of soup and love, the first is best."—*Spanish proverb*
"Worries go down better with soup."—*Yiddish proverb*

11

"FLOATING" HOLIDAYS THIS MONTH

Man Watchers Week second week, Sunday thru Saturday

International Printing Week third week, Sunday thru Saturday
Punctuation was not used until the advent of printing in the fifteenth century. Before that, wordswerewrittenbyhandandruntogetherlikethis.

Martin Luther King Day observed in United States on the third Monday
"Human salvation lies in the hands of the creatively maladjusted."—*Martin Luther King, Jr., American clergyman and civil rights leader, born Jan 15, 1929*

Printing Ink Day third Tuesday
"Say it with flowers, say it with eats.
Say it with kisses, say it with sweets.
Say it with jewelry, say it with drink,
But always be careful not to say it with ink."—*Anon.*

Hat Day third Friday
"The way to fight a woman is with your hat—grab it and run."
—*John Barrymore*

Spouse's Day fourth Friday
"Marriage is the only life sentence that can be commuted for bad behavior."—*Anon.*

"Of course a platonic relationship is possible—but only between husband and wife."—*Ladies' Home Journal*

"To make a happy couple, the husband must be deaf and the wife blind."—*French proverb*

"Before going to war say one prayer, before going to sea, two, and before getting married, three."—*Polish proverb*

"Marriage is the only war in which you sleep with the enemy."—*Anon.*

"The most dangerous food is wedding cake."—*Anon.*

"Alimony: The billing without the cooing."—*Anon.*

Super Bowl usually third or fourth Sunday in Jan or first Sunday in Feb
"Football's not a matter of life and death. It's much more serious than that."—*Bill Shankly (biographical information not available)*

JANUARY 1

Happy New Year
New Year's is the world's most widely celebrated holiday.

The "toast" had its origin in Rome, where a bit of spiced, burned bread was put into the wine to improve the flavor and absorb the sediment. The drink itself became a "toast," as did the gesture of drinking to a friend's good health.

"I've drunk your health in company,
I've drunk your health alone;
I've drunk your health so many times,
I've damn near ruined my own."—*Anon.*

E(dward) M(organ) Forster, *English novelist, born Jan 1, 1879*
"How can I think till I see what I say?"

J(erome) D(avid) Salinger, *American novelist and short-story writer, born Jan 1, 1919*
"I am a kind of paranoiac in reverse. I suspect people of plotting to make me happy."

JANUARY 2

Break Your New Year's Resolution Day
"If at first you don't succeed, destroy all evidence that you tried."—*Anon.*

"I never have frustrations.
The reason is to wit:
If at first I don't succeed,
I quit!"—*Anon.*

Samuel Diamond, *American accountant, born Jan 2, 1931*
"The greatest distance between two points is between where your mouth is and where your money is."

JANUARY 3

United States Congress assembles
"If the opposite of 'pro' is 'con,' then what is the opposite of progress?"—*Anon.*

"Congress is so strange. A man gets up to speak and says nothing. Nobody listens—and then everybody disagrees."—*Boris Marshalov, American actor, born 1902 (birth date not available)*

Clement (Richard) Attlee, *English politician and Prime Minister, born Jan 3, 1883*
"Mr. Attlee is a modest man. But then he has much to be modest about."—*Winston Churchill about Clement Attlee*

"The House of Lords is like a glass of champagne that has stood for five days."

"Democracy means government by discussion, but it is only effective if you can stop people talking."

On himself: "Few thought him ever a starter
There were many who thought themselves smarter
But he ended PM, CH and OM
An Earl and a Knight of the Garter."

Victor Borge, *American pianist and comedian, born Borge Rosenbaum, Jan 3, 1909*
"When an opera star sings her head off, she usually improves her appearance."

Victoria Principal, *American actress, born Jan 3, 1945*
"I don't know how it happens. My car just drives itself to Neiman-Marcus."

JANUARY 4

Trivia Day
A United States government survey, accomplished for a mere $50,000, determined that the average length of a stewardess's nose was 2.6 inches.

Goodyear Rubber Company in 1978 reported that decades of research had produced an absolute conclusion that shoes on right feet wear out faster than shoes on left feet.

(Sir) Isaac Newton, *English physicist, mathematician and philosopher, born Jan 4, 1643*
"I do not know what I may appear to the world. But, to myself, I seem to have been only like a boy playing on the seashore, diverting myself in now and then finding a smoother pebble or a prettier shell than the ordinary, whilst the great ocean of truth lay all undiscovered before me."

Louis Braille, *French teacher and musician (inventor of the Braille system), born Jan 4, 1809*

"On the chest of a barmaid in Sale
Were tattooed the prices of ale,
And on her behind,
For the sake of the blind,
Was the same information in Braille."—*Anon.*

Everett M(cKinley) Dirksen, *American businessman, lawyer and politician, born Jan 4, 1896*
"A billion here, a billion there—pretty soon it adds up to real money."

Maureen Reagan, *American politician (daughter of 40th US President), born Jan 4, 1941*
"I will feel equality has arrived when we can elect to office women who are as incompetent as some of the men who are already there."

JANUARY 5

Predict the Future Day
   Jeane (Pinckert) Dixon, *American clairvoyant, astrologer, colum-*
nist and writer, born Jan 5, 1918

All of us at some time have wished that we could predict the future.
Here are some unusual methods you might want to try: *austro-
mancy,* by the winds (hoping an ill one isn't blowing?), *moleosophy,*
by moles on the body (someone else's, we hope), *onychomancy,* by
fingernails (doesn't sound like as much fun as the last one), *gyro-
mancy,* by whirling around until dizziness causes a fall (but what if
you're too dizzy to remember?), and *geoloscopy,* by a person's manner of laughing (but when that's happening, why worry about the
future?).

"Perhaps the best thing about the future is that it only comes one
day at a time."—*Anon.*

JANUARY 6

Carl Sandburg, *American poet, biographer and historian, born
Jan 6, 1878*

"The cruelest thing that has happened to Lincoln since he was shot
by Booth was to fall into the hands of Carl Sandburg."—*Edmund
Wilson about Carl Sandburg*

"Here is the difference between Dante, Milton and me. They wrote
about hell and never saw the place. I wrote about Chicago after
looking the place over for years and years."

"I am an idealist. I don't know where I'm going but I'm on my way."

Joey Adams, *American comedian, born Jan 6, 1911*
"The most popular labor-saving device today is still a husband with
money."

"Never let a fool kiss you or a kiss fool you."

"Marriage is give and take. You'd better give it to her or she'll take
it anyway."

"A genius is one who can do anything except make a living."

"Science is really going at a rapid pace. Now it's only a hundred
years behind the comic strips."

Loretta Young, *American actress, born Gretchen Young, Jan 6, 1912*
"If you want a place in the sun, you have to expect a few blisters."

JANUARY 7

(Lord) Gordon Hewart, *English jurist, born Jan 7, 1870*
"The only impartiality possible to the human mind is that which arises from understanding neither side of the case."

Adolph Zukor, *American entrepreneur and film executive, born Jan 7, 1873*
At age 99: "If I'd known how old I was going to be I'd have taken better care of myself."

Walter Davenport, *American journalist, editor and writer, born Jan 7, 1889*
"An editor is a person who knows precisely what he wants but isn't quite sure."

Scott (Bowen) Elledge, *American educator, born Jan 7, 1914*
On his retirement from Cornell: "It is time I stepped aside for a less experienced and less able man."

JANUARY 8

Elvis (Aron) Presley, *American singer and actor, born Jan 8, 1935*
"I don't know anything about music. In my line you don't have to."
In 1955 he was rejected by Arthur Godfrey's Talent Scouts.

JANUARY 9

Richard M(ilhous) Nixon, *American lawyer, politician, 36th US Vice President and 37th US President, born Jan 9, 1913*
"I'll speak for the man, or against him, whichever will do him the most good."

"I would have made a good Pope."

"I would not like to be a political leader in Russia. They never know when they're being taped."

Gypsy Rose Lee, *American striptease artist and novelist, born Rose Louise Hovick, Jan 9, 1914*
"She's descended from a long line her mother listened to."

"Royalties are nice and all but shaking the beads brings in money quicker."

"I have everything now I had twenty years ago—except it's all lower."

"Men aren't attracted to me by my mind. They're attracted by what I don't mind."

JANUARY 10

Find the Top of Your Desk Day

We've had "Dress for Success" and "Stress for Success," but here's a new one on us—"Mess for Success." Messiness, we're told, breeds creativity, saves time (the time we'd otherwise spend getting organized), and keeps us from being intimidating by being too perfect. Not only that, messy people have more confidence and thus don't need to be very organized to feel in control. (Guess next time we're caught straightening our desks, we'll be demoted.)

Find the Top of Your Desk Day

JANUARY 11

William James, *American teacher, philosopher, psychologist and writer, born Jan 11, 1842*

"Language is the most imperfect and expensive means yet discovered for communicating thought."

"There is only one thing a philosopher can be relied on to do, and that is to contradict other philosophers."

JANUARY 12

Handwriting Day
John Hancock, *American patriot and statesman (first signer of Declaration of Independence), born Jan 12, 1737*

"Doctors really must get typewriters. This lady is suffering from something unreadable."—*Tudor Rees, English magistrate (birth date not available)*

"Texas" (Mary Louise Cecilia) Guinan, *American actress and night-club hostess, born Jan 12, 1884*

"A politician is a fellow who will lay down your life for his country."

Joe E. Lewis, *American actor and comedian, born Jan 12, 1902*

"I always wake up at the crack of ice."

"Henny" (Henry) Youngman, *American comedian and actor, born Jan 12, 1906*

"My wife is a light eater ... as soon as it's light, she starts to eat."

"My grandmother is over eighty and still doesn't need glasses. Drinks right out of the bottle."

JANUARY 13

Sophie Tucker, *American singer, born Sophie Abuza, Jan 13, 1884*

"From birth to age 18, a girl needs good parents, from 18 to 35 she needs good looks, from 35 to 55 she needs a good personality, and from 55 on she needs cash."

"I have been poor and I have been rich. Rich is better."

JANUARY 14

"Andy" (Andrew Aitken) Rooney, *American columnist, writer and curmudgeon, born Jan 14, 1919*

"Crossing the street in New York keeps old people young—if they make it."

"The two biggest sellers in any bookstore are the cookbooks and the diet books. The cookbooks tell you how to prepare the food and the diet books tell you how not to eat any of it."

Martin (Prager) Mayer, *American journalist, editor, novelist and writer, born Jan 14, 1928*

"Except for the con men borrowing money they shouldn't get and the widows who have to visit with the handsome young men in the trust department, no sane person ever enjoyed visiting a bank."

JANUARY 15

Molière, *French playwright, born Jean-Baptiste Poquelin, Jan 15, 1622*
"It infuriates me to be wrong when I know I'm right."

Goodman Ace, *American writer and actor, born Jan 15, 1899*
"The best cure for hypochondria is to forget about your body and get interested in somebody else's."

"Politics makes estranged bedfellows."

"Take anything any doctor says with a grain of aspirin."

"Familiarity breeds attempt."

"I keep reading between the lies."

Frank (Henry) Westheimer, *American chemist and teacher, born Jan 15, 1912*
"A couple of months in the laboratory can frequently save a couple of hours in the library."

JANUARY 16

Nothing Day
Don't celebrate, observe or honor anything.

(Federico) De Roberto, *Italian journalist, short-story writer, novelist and critic, born Jan 16, 1861*
"Among all human constructions the only ones that avoid the dissolving sands of time are castles in the air."

"Dizzy" (Jay Hanna) Dean, *American baseball player and sports announcer, born Jan 16, 1911*
"Me and [my brother] Paul didn't get much education."

JANUARY 17

Benjamin Franklin, *American statesman, printer, writer, scientist and inventor, born Jan 17, 1706*
"If you would know the value of money, go and try to borrow some."

"He that falls in love with himself will have no rivals."

"Rich widows are the only secondhand goods that sell at first-class prices."

David Lloyd George, *English statesman and Prime Minister, born Jan 17, 1863*

Don't celebrate, observe or honor anything.

"He could not see a belt without hitting below it."—*Margot Asquith about David Lloyd George*

"He spent his whole life in plastering together the true and the false and therefrom extracting the plausible."—*Stanley Baldwin about David Lloyd George*

"A master of improvised speech and improvised policies."—*A.J.P. Taylor about David Lloyd George*

"A politician is a person with whose politics you don't agree; if you agree with him he is a statesman."

"Count not my broken pledges as a crime, I *meant* them, *how* I meant them, at the time."

At the World War I Peace Conference, he told the Italians to boost their banana crop as a means of reviving their economy. Tripling it wouldn't have helped, though, as Italy did not grow bananas.

"Al" (Alphonse) Capone, *American gangster, born Jan 17, 1899*
    "I don't even know what street Canada is on."

"Vote early and vote often."

"Don't get the idea that I'm knocking the American system."

Newton (Norman) Minow, *American lawyer and head of US Federal Communications Commission, born Jan 17, 1926*
"The past is not always worse than the present."

Muhammad Ali, *American boxer, born Cassius Marcellus Clay, Jr., Jan 17, 1942*
"He stings like a bee but lives like a WASP."—*Eamonn Andrews about Muhammad Ali*

"My toughest fight was with my first wife."

"I have said I am the greatest. Ain't nobody ever heard me say I was the smartest."

JANUARY 18

Oh Pooh Day
   A(lan) A(lexander) Milne, *English children's author, playwright, essayist and poet, born Jan 18, 1882*
   "Of course, it is quite possible to marry for love, but I suspect that a good many bachelors marry so that they may not have to bother about the washing any more. That, anyhow, will be one of the reasons with me. 'I offer you,' I shall say, 'my hand and heart—*and* the washing.' "

Cary Grant, *English actor, born Archibald Alexander Leach, Jan 18, 1904*
   "Divorce is a game played by lawyers."

   "When I am married, I want to be single, and when I am single, I want to be married."

   "All my wives were my favorites."

   "I improve on misquotation."

Danny Kaye, *American actor and comedian, born David Daniel Kaminski, Jan 18, 1913*
   "If there is a dispute between a musician and myself, it is settled amicably. I win."

JANUARY 19

Confederate Heroes Day in United States
   Robert E(dward) Lee, *American Confederate military leader, born Jan 19, 1807 and*
   Dolly (Rebecca) Parton, *American singer, songwriter, musician and actress, born Jan 19, 1946*

"You'd be surprised how much it costs to look this cheap."
—*Dolly Parton*

Edgar Allan Poe, *American poet, short-story writer and critic, born Jan 19, 1809*
"I have great faith in fools; self-confidence my friends call it."

Alexander Woollcott, *American actor, journalist and critic, born Jan 19, 1887*
"The scenery was beautiful, but the actors got in front of it."

"The English have an extraordinary ability for flying into a great calm."

JANUARY 20

Richard Le Gallienne, *English poet and essayist, born Jan 20, 1866*
"A critic is a man created to praise greater men than himself, but he is never able to find them."

George Burns, *American actor and comedian, born Nathan Birnbaum, Jan 20, 1896*
"Happiness is having a large, loving, caring, close-knit family in another city."

"There were twelve kids in my family, and my mother's idea of liberation was to get *into* the kitchen."

"Retirement at sixty-five is ridiculous. When I was sixty-five I still had pimples."

"It's hard for me to get used to these changing times. I can remember when the air was clean and sex was dirty."

"Smartness runs in my family. When I went to school I was so smart my teacher was in my class for five years."

"I was married by a judge. I should have asked for a jury."

"I smoke cigars because at my age if I don't have something to hang onto I might fall down."

JANUARY 21

Hugging Day
"Hugging is a means of getting two people so close together that they can't see anything wrong with each other."—*Anon.*

Speak Your Mind Day
Roger Nash Baldwin, *American lawyer and social activist (founder of American Civil Liberties Union), born Jan 21, 1884*
"Talk is cheap because supply exceeds demand."—Anon.

"A narrow mind and a wide mouth usually go together."—*Anon.*

Christian Dior, *French fashion designer, born Jan 21, 1905*
"Women are most fascinating between the ages of thirty-five and forty, after they have won a few races and know how to pace themselves. Since few women ever pass forty, maximum fascination can continue indefinitely."

JANUARY 22

(Sir) Francis Bacon, *English statesman and writer, born Jan 22, 1561*

"When their lordships asked Bacon
How many bribes he had taken
He had at least the grace
To get very red in the face."—*Hilaire Belloc about Francis Bacon*

"Hope is a good breakfast, but it is a bad supper."

(Lord) George Gordon (Noel) Byron, *English poet, born Jan 22, 1788*

"All human history attests
That happiness for man—the hungry sinner!
Since Eve ate apples, much depends on dinner."

"Now hatred is by far the longest pleasure;
Men love in haste, but they detest at leisure."

(Johan) August Strindberg, *Swedish playwright, novelist and short-story writer, born Jan 22, 1849*
"I loathe people who keep dogs. They are cowards who haven't got the guts to bite people themselves."

John Russell, *English art historian, columnist and critic, born Jan 22, 1919*
On modern European hotels: "The bedrooms are just large enough for a well-behaved dwarf and a greyhound on a diet."

JANUARY 23

Jeanne Moreau, *French actress, born Jan 23, 1928*
"To age well it helps to have two things: fame and money."

JANUARY 24

William Congreve, *English playwright, born Jan 24, 1670*
"... I keep the commandments, I love my neighbour as my selfe, and to avoid Coveting my neighbour's wife I desire to be coveted by her: which you know is quite another thing."

Vicki Baum, *American novelist and playwright, born Jan 24, 1896*
"Marriage always demands the greatest understanding of the art of insincerity possible between two human beings."

Yakov Smirnoff, *American comedian, born Jan 24, 1951*
"In America, you can always find a party. In Russia, the party always finds you."

JANUARY 25

W(illiam) Somerset Maugham, *English novelist, playwright and short-story writer, born Jan 25, 1874*
"It is very unfair to expect a politician to live in private up to the statements he makes in public."

"There are three rules for writing a novel. Unfortunately, no one knows what they are."

"The unfortunate thing about this world is that good habits are so much easier to give up than bad ones."

"American women expect to find in their husbands a perfection that English women only hope to find in their butlers."

"Impropriety is the soul of wit."

"Love is what happens to men and women who don't know each other."

"Excess on occasion is exhilarating. It prevents moderation from acquiring the deadly effect of habit."

"She's too crafty a woman to invent a new lie when an old one will serve."

"There is only one thing about which I am certain, and that is that there is very little about which one can be certain."

"I was a good young man and I'm glad to say it's enabled me to be a wicked old one."

Virginia Woolf, *English novelist and essayist, born Adeline Virginia Stephen, Jan 25, 1882*
"Women have served all these centuries as looking-glasses possessing the magic and delicious power of reflecting the figure of man at twice its natural size."

JANUARY 26

Paul Newman, *American actor, director, producer and race-car driver, born Jan 26, 1925*
"I have often thought it might very well appear in my obituary or on my tombstone or somewhere that 'Here lies Paul Newman who died a complete failure because his eyes suddenly turned brown.'"

Jules Feiffer, *American cartoonist, editor and playwright, born Jan 26, 1929*
"Getting out of bed in the morning is an act of false confidence."

JANUARY 27

Lewis Carroll, *English mathematician, writer and children's author, born Charles Lutwidge Dodgson, Jan 27, 1832*
"Sometimes I've believed as many as six impossible things before breakfast."

(Friedrich) Wilhelm (Viktor Albert) II, *German emperor, born Jan 27, 1859*
"He can be most fascinating, and win hearts wherever he goes—and doesn't stay."—*Count Paul Waldersee about Wilhelm II*

Hyman (George) Rickover, *American naval officer, engineer and physicist, born Jan 27, 1900*
"To increase the efficiency of the Department of Defense, you must first abolish it."

Mordecai Richler, *Canadian novelist, short-story writer and journalist, born Jan 27, 1931*
"Wherever I travel, I'm too late. The orgy has moved elsewhere."

JANUARY 28

(Sidonie-Gabrielle) Colette, *French novelist, born Jan 28, 1873*
"When one can read ... why write?"

Artur Rubenstein, *American pianist, born Jan 28, 1887*
At age 90: "Sometimes I think, not so much am I a pianist, but a vampire. All my life I have lived off the blood of Chopin."

JANUARY 29

Anton (Pavlovich) Chekhov, *Russian playwright and short-story writer, born Jan 29, 1860*
"If you are afraid of loneliness, don't marry."

W.C. Fields, *American actor and comedian, born Claude William Dukenfield, Jan 29, 1880*
"Reminds me of my safari in Africa. Somebody forgot the corkscrew and for several days we had to live on nothing but food and water."

"All my available funds are completely tied up in ready cash."

"Inflation has gone up over a dollar a quart."

"If at first you don't succeed, try, try again. Then give up. No use being a damn fool about it."

"Somebody left the cork out of my lunch."

"Start every day off with a smile and get it over with."

"Women are like elephants to me: I like to look at them, but I wouldn't want to own one."

"I was in love with a beautiful blonde once—she drove me to drink—'tis the one thing I'm indebted to her for."

"A thing worth having is a thing worth cheating for."

"A wonderful drink, wine.... Did you ever hear of an Italian grape crusher with athlete's foot?"

"Anybody who hates children and dogs can't be all bad."

"I always keep a supply of stimulant handy in case I see a snake— which I also keep handy."

"I got Mark Hellinger so drunk last night that it took three bellboys to put me to bed."

"I went to Philadelphia one Sunday. The place was closed."

"Never give a sucker an even break."

Asked if he favored clubs for women: "Indubitably. But only if every other form of persuasion fails."

"I can lick my weight in wildflowers."

"I am free of all prejudice. I hate everyone equally."

Victor Mature, *American actor, born Jan 29, 1916*
"Actually, I am a golfer.... I never was an actor; ask anybody, particularly the critics."

N(orman) F(rederick) Simpson, *English teacher, playwright and screenwriter, born Jan 29, 1919*
"I eat merely to put food out of my mind."

JANUARY 30

Franklin D(elano) Roosevelt, *American lawyer, politician and 32nd US President, born Jan 30, 1882*
"The man who started more creations than were ever begun since Genesis—and finished none."—*Hugh Johnson about Franklin D. Roosevelt*

"One-third mush and two-thirds Eleanor."—*Alice Roosevelt Longworth about Franklin D. Roosevelt*

"A radical is a man with both feet planted firmly in the air."

"I belong to Bridegrooms Anonymous. Whenever I feel like getting married, they send over a lady in a house-coat and hair curlers to burn my toast for me."

"A man who has never gone to school may steal from a freight car, but if he has a university education, he may steal the whole railroad."

Dick Martin, *American comedian, born Jan 30, 1923*
"I belong to Bridegrooms Anonymous. Whenever I feel like getting married, they send over a lady in a housecoat and hair curlers to burn my toast for me."

JANUARY 31

Eddie Cantor, *American actor and comedian, born Edward Israel Iskowitz, Jan 31, 1892*
"The two most common causes of divorce? Men and women."

"I know one star in Hollywood who hasn't been spoiled by success, and that is Mickey Mouse."

Tallulah (Brockman) Bankhead, *American actress, born Jan 31, 1903*
"Tallulah is always skating on thin ice. Everyone wants to be there when it breaks."—*Mrs. Patrick Campbell about Tallulah Bankhead*

"Nobody can be exactly like me. Sometimes even I have trouble doing it."

About a part she once refused to play: "There is less in this than meets the eye."

"It's the good girls who keep the diaries, the bad girls never have the time."

"The only thing I regret about my past is the length of it. If I had to live my life again I'd make the same mistakes, only sooner."

"I am as pure as the driven slush."

Norman Mailer, *American novelist, journalist and writer, born Jan 31, 1923*
"You don't know anything about a woman until you meet her in court."

"If a person is not talented enough to be a novelist, not smart enough to be a lawyer, and his hands are too shaky to perform operations, he becomes a journalist."

Suzanne Pleshette, *American actress, born Jan 31, 1937*
"If God had wanted me to exercise, I'd have been born with a Nautilus machine attached!"

February

American Heart Month

"The most serious charge which can be brought against New England is not Puritanism but February."—*Joseph Wood Krutch*

American Heart Month

"Cardiologists don't really need to give stress tests and EKGs. They can check the condition of a patient's heart just by sending him a bill."—*Anon.*

National Meat Month
"Culture is what your butcher would have if he were a surgeon."
—*Mary Pettibone Poole (biographical information not available)*

International Friendship Month
"The only man who sticks closer to you in adversity than a friend is a creditor."—*Anon.*

"A friend in need is a friend to dodge."—*Anon.*

"A real friend is someone who takes a winter vacation on a sun-drenched beach and doesn't send a card."—*Farmer's Almanac*

"There is nothing more friendly than a friend in need."
—*Plautus, Roman playwright*

"Real friends are those who, when you've made a fool of yourself, don't feel you've done a permanent job."—*Anon.*

"Seeing ourselves as others see us would probably confirm our worst suspicions about them."—*Franklin P. Jones, American attorney, born 1906 (birth date not available)*

"FLOATING" HOLIDAYS THIS MONTH

Presidents' Day observed in United States third Monday
"People, like sheep, tend to follow a leader—occasionally in the right direction."—*Alexander Chase (biographical information not available)*

FEBRUARY 1

National Freedom Day in United States
13th Amendment, abolishing slavery, approved by President Abraham Lincoln Feb 1, 1865

Marriage: "The state or condition of a community consisting of a master, a mistress and two slaves, making two in all."
—*Ambrose Bierce*

Robinson Crusoe Day a day to be adventurous and self-reliant.

Alexander Selkirk, Scottish sailor, was rescued February 1, 1709 from island Juan Fernandez after being left there in September 1704 at his own request after an argument with his captain. (Suppose he had enough time to "find" his temper?)

Richard Whately, *English clergyman and educator, born Feb 1, 1787*
"Never argue at the dinner table, for the one who is not hungry always gets the best of the argument."

(William) Clark Gable, *American actor, born Feb 1, 1901*
   "Talent is the least important thing a performer needs...."

S(idney) J(oseph) Perelman, *American short-story writer, screen-writer and humorist, born Feb 1, 1904*
   "A farm is an irregular patch of nettles, bound by short term notes, containing a fool and his wife who didn't know enough to stay in the city."

FEBRUARY 2

Ground-Hog Day
   "A ground hog is a furry critter
   Deep in the earth he breeds his litter
   On February 2 he checks out the sun
   If he sees his shadow, winter ain't done—
   Six more weeks he's a baby sitter."—*Bruce Dexter*

(Charles-Maurice de) Talleyrand(-Périgord), *French statesman and diplomat, born Feb 2, 1754*
   "Mistrust first impulses, they are always good."

(Henry) Havelock Ellis, *English essayist, editor and physician, born Feb 2, 1859*
   "What we call progress is the exchange of one nuisance for another nuisance."
   "A man must not swallow more beliefs than he can digest."

James (Augustine Aloysius) Joyce, *Irish novelist and poet, born Feb 2, 1882*
   "A man of genius makes no mistakes. His errors are volitional and are portals of discovery."
   "If I can throw any obscurity on the subject, let me know."

Jascha Heifetz, *American violinist, born Feb 2, 1901*
   "One Russian is an anarchist
   Two Russians are a chess game
   Three Russians are a revolution
   Four Russians are the Budapest String Quartet."
   "No matter what side of an argument you're on, you always find some people on your side that you wish were on the other side."
   "I occasionally play works by contemporary composers, and for two reasons. First, to discourage the composer from writing any more, and secondly to remind myself how much I appreciate Beethoven."

Harold Rosenberg, *American teacher, philosopher, poet, translator, writer and critic, born Feb 2, 1906*

"No degree of dullness can safeguard a work against the determination of critics to find it fascinating."

"An artist is a person who has invented an artist."

FEBRUARY 3

Horace Greeley, *American editor and politician, born Feb 3, 1811*

To a Congressman who described himself as a "self-made man":
"That, sir, relieves the Almighty of a great responsibility."

Gertrude Stein, *American novelist, short-story writer, poet and essayist, born Feb 3, 1874*

"While she believed that most writers failed to allow writing to express all that it could, in her own practice she scrupulously saw to it that writing expressed less than it would."—*John Malcolm Brinnin about Gertrude Stein*

"Miss Stein was a past master in making nothing happen very slowly."—*Clifton Fadiman about Gertrude Stein*

"Money is always there, but the pockets change."

Shelley Berman, *American comedian, born Feb 3, 1926*

On getting to the airport in time: "The sooner you are there, the sooner you will find out how long you will be delayed."

Victor Buono, *American actor, born Feb 3, 1938*

"My only aversion to vice,
Is the price."

FEBRUARY 4

Don't Diet Day

"Never eat more than you can lift."—*Miss Piggy, Muppet actress*

"Eat, drink, and be merry, for tomorrow we diet."—*Anon.*

"Diet: penalty for exceeding the feed limit."—*Anon.*

"God must have loved calories because He made so many of them."—*Anon.*

"Americans like fat books and thin women."—*Anon.*

A 250-pound, self-described "80's woman" who doesn't stand for any nonsense keeps an enormous assortment of candies in her office. Her explanation? "I'm on a weight-maintenance program."

Merely resting comfortably, the average person burns up 1700 calories in twenty-four hours.

FEBRUARY 5

(Sir) Robert Peel, *English politician and Prime Minister, born Feb 5, 1788*

"Public opinion is a compound of folly, weakness, prejudice, wrong feeling, right feeling, obstinacy, and newspaper paragraphs."

Adlai Ewing Stevenson (II), *American lawyer, politician and diplomat, born Feb 5, 1900*

"Man does not live by words alone, despite the fact that sometimes he has to eat them."

"A politician is a man who approaches every question with an open mouth."

"A diplomat's life is made up of three ingredients: protocol, Geritol, and alcohol."

"An editor is one who separates the wheat from the chaff and prints the chaff."

"Power corrupts, but lack of power corrupts absolutely."

"In America any boy may become President, and I suppose that's just the risk he takes."

"The hardest thing about any political campaign is how to win without proving that you are unworthy of winning."

"A lie is an abomination unto the Lord and a very present help in trouble."

William (Seward) Burroughs, *American novelist, born Feb 5, 1914*

"A paranoid is a man who knows a little of what's going on."

FEBRUARY 6

Ronald (Wilson) Reagan, *American actor, businessman, writer, politician and 40th US President, born Feb 6, 1911*

"Ronald Reagan is not a typical politician because he doesn't know how to lie, cheat, and steal. He's always had an agent for that."
—*Bob Hope about Ronald Reagan*

"In a disastrous fire in President Reagan's library both books were destroyed. And the real tragedy is that he hadn't finished colouring one."—*Jonathan Hunt about Ronald Reagan*

"Reagan is proof that there is life after death."—*Mort Sahl about Ronald Reagan*

On hearing that Reagan was elected governor of California: "It's our fault. We should have given him better parts."—*Jack Warner about Ronald Reagan*

In 1973: "The thought of being President frightens me and I do not think I want the job."

"I used to say that politics was the second lowest profession and I have come to know that it bears a great similarity to the first."

"The best minds are not in government. If any were, business would hire them away."

"The nine most terrifying words in the English language are, 'I'm from the government and I'm here to help.' "

"I have left orders to be awakened at any time in case of national emergency, even if I'm in a cabinet meeting."

Zsa Zsa (Sari) Gabor, *Hungarian actress, born Feb 6, 1919*
"Every woman in Beverly Hills is wondering what to get her husband for Christmas. Zsa Zsa Gabor is wondering what husband to get for Christmas."—*Milton Berle about Zsa Zsa Gabor*

"All a man really wants is complete worship and adoration. He knows he's perfect, but he likes to hear it from you."

"Husbands are like fires. They go out if unattended."

"A girl must marry for love, and keep on marrying until she finds it."

"A man in love is incomplete until he is married. Then he is finished."

"There's really nothing wrong with a woman welcoming all men's advances, darling, as long as they are in cash."

"Conrad Hilton and I had one thing in common. We both wanted his money."

"I never hated a man enough to give him his diamonds back."

"I'm a wonderful housekeeper. Every time I get a divorce, I keep the house."

Denis Norden, *English scriptwriter and broadcaster, born Feb 6, 1922*
"There was only one occasion in my life when I put myself on a strict diet and I can tell you, hand on heart, it was the most miserable afternoon I have ever spent."

FEBRUARY 7

(Harry) Sinclair Lewis, *American novelist, born Feb 7, 1885*
"People will buy anything that's one to a customer."

On May 5, 1926 he declined the Pulitzer Prize, saying that such prizes tend to make writers "safe, polite, obedient and sterile." He accepted the Nobel Prize for Literature in 1930.

FEBRUARY 8

Lana Turner, *American actress, born Julia Jean Mildred Frances Turner, Feb 8, 1921*
> "A successful man is one who makes more money than his wife can spend. A successful woman is one who can find such a man."

> "There's something awfully compelling about a large engagement ring."

> "How does it happen that something that makes so much sense in the moonlight doesn't make any sense at all in the sunlight?"

James (Byron) Dean, *American actor, born Feb 8, 1931*
> "I act for the same reason most actors act, to express the fantasies in which I have involved myself."

FEBRUARY 9

George Ade, *American journalist, playwright and humorist, born Feb 9, 1866*
> "Early to bed and early to rise, and you'll meet very few of our best people."

> "Anyone can win, unless there happens to be a second entry."

> "Her features did not seem to know the value of teamwork."

FEBRUARY 10

Charles Lamb, *English essayist, poet and critic, born Feb 10, 1775*
> "I am determined my children shall be brought up in their father's religion, if they can find out what it is."

(Maurice) Harold Macmillan, *English statesman and Prime Minister, born Feb 10, 1894*
> "Diplomacy is forever poised between a cliché and an indiscretion."

> "If, like me, you are over 90, frail, on two sticks, half deaf and half blind, you stick out like a sore thumb in most places, but not in the House of Lords."

> "I am MacWonder one moment and MacBlunder the next."

Bertolt Brecht, *German poet and playwright, born Eugen Berthold Friedrich Brecht, Feb 10, 1898*
> "I don't trust him. We're friends."

> "Whenever there are tremendous virtues it's a sure sign something's wrong."

> "Life is short and so is money."

> "Grub first, then ethics."

On leaner beef: "Before long it will be the animals who do the dieting so that the ultimate consumer does not have to."

Mimi Sheraton, *American food writer and critic, born Feb 10, 1926*
On leaner beef: "Before long it will be the animals who do the dieting so that the ultimate consumer does not have to."

FEBRUARY 11

Inventor's Day
"The marvels of modern technology include the development of a soda can which, when discarded, will last forever, and a $7,000 car which, when properly cared for, will rust out in two or three years."—*Paul Harwitz (biographical information not available)*

Thomas (Alva) Edison, *American inventor, born Feb 11, 1847*
"When down in the mouth, remember Jonah. He came out all right."

At age six, he came home from school one day with a note from his teacher suggesting he be taken out of school because he was "too stupid to learn."

Farouk I, *Egyptian king, born Feb 11, 1920*
On being deposed: "There will soon be only five kings left: the Kings of England, Diamonds, Hearts, Spades and Clubs."

Gary North, *American economist and writer, born Feb 11, 1942*
"Some extremely sharp investment advisors can get you in at the bottom of the market. Some extremely sharp ones can get you out at the top. They are never the same people."

FEBRUARY 12

Abraham Lincoln, *American lawyer, politician and 16th US President, born Feb 12, 1809*
"He can compress the most words into the smallest idea of any man I ever met."

"I was told I was on the road to hell, but I had no idea it was just a mile down the road with a Dome on it."

"It has been my experience that folks who have no vices have very few virtues."

"A woman is the only thing I am afraid of that I know will not hurt me."

"Tact is the ability to describe others as they see themselves."

"Better to remain silent and be thought a fool than to speak out and remove all doubt."

"If this is coffee, please bring me some tea; if this is tea, please bring me some coffee."

"If I were two-faced, would I be wearing this one?"

Alice Roosevelt Longworth, *American socialite, born Feb 12, 1884*
"If you haven't got anything nice to say about anybody, come sit next to me."

George Mikes, *English journalist, editor, writer and humorist, born Feb 12, 1912*
"English humour resembles the Loch Ness Monster in that both are famous but there is a strong suspicion that neither exists."

"The criterion of a gentleman is that however poor he may be he still refuses to do useful work."

FEBRUARY 13

(Lord) Randolph (Henry Spencer) Churchill, *English politician, born Feb 13, 1849*
"Dear Randolph, utterly unspoiled by failure."—*Noel Coward about Randolph Churchill*

George Segal, *American actor, born Feb 13, 1934*
"The good thing about the movies is that you can eat and meditate at the same time."

FEBRUARY 14

Valentine's Day
"If it's not till Spring that a young man's fancy turns to love, what is it he's got in mind on Valentine's Day?"—*Bruce Dexter*

Frank Harris, *American editor, journalist, biographer and novelist, born James Thomas Harris, Feb 14, 1856*
"Frank Harris is invited to all the great houses in England—once."—*Oscar Wilde about Frank Harris*

George Jean Nathan, *American editor, drama critic and writer, born Feb 14, 1882*
"Hollywood impresses me as being ten million dollars' worth of intricate and highly ingenious machinery functioning elaborately to put skin on baloney."

"Marriage is based on the theory that when a man discovers a brand of beer exactly to his taste he should at once throw up his job and go to work in the brewery."

"My interest in the cinema has lapsed since women began to talk."

"A poet is simply an alchemist who transmutes his cynicism regarding human beings into an optimism regarding the moon, the stars, the heavens, and the flowers, to say nothing of spring."

Love: "An emotion experienced by the many and enjoyed by the few."

"I drink to make other people more interesting."

Jack Benny, *American actor and comedian, born Benjamin Kubelsky, Feb 14, 1894*
"Mary and I have been married forty-seven years, and not once have we ever had an argument serious enough to mention the word divorce ... murder, yes, but divorce, never."

"It's absolutely true. I don't want to tell you how much insurance I carry with Prudential, but all I can say is—when I go, they go."

"Jimmy" (James Riddle) Hoffa, *American labor leader, born Feb 14, 1913*
"I may have my faults, but being wrong ain't one of them."

FEBRUARY 15

Jeremy Bentham, *English economist and philosopher, born Feb 15, 1748*

"Lawyers are the only persons in whom ignorance of the law is not punished."

John Barrymore, *American actor, born Feb 15, 1882*
"You never realize how short a month is until you pay alimony."

"The trouble with life is that there are so many beautiful women—and so little time."

"It will be impossible for me to accept because of a previous engagement, which I shall make as soon as possible."

"There are three things a woman can make out of almost anything—a salad, a hat, and a quarrel."

Jane Seymour, *English actress, born Joyce Frankenberg, Feb 15, 1951*
On American men: "They have wonderful minds. So much is stored inside—all those sports scores and so on."

FEBRUARY 16

Critics' Day
Ivor Armstrong Richards, *English writer, poet, teacher and critic (the "critic's critic"), born Feb 16, 1893*
"Honest criticism is hard to take, particularly from a relative, a friend, an acquaintance, or a stranger."—*Franklin P. Jones, American attorney, born 1906 (birth date not available)*

"Most of us would rather be ruined by praise than saved by criticism."—*Anon.*

Henry Brooks Adams, *American historian and writer, born Feb 16, 1838*
"Philosophy gives us unintelligible answers to insoluble problems."

Wayne ("The Waltz King") King, *American band leader, born Feb 16, 1901*
On Bisbee, Arizona: "It is a picture postcard lost for eight decades in the mail."

Edgar Bergen, *American entertainer and ventriloquist, born Edgar John Bergren, Feb 16, 1903*
"Hard work never killed anybody, but why take a chance?"
—*Charlie McCarthy, sidekick of Edgar Bergen*

FEBRUARY 17

Advertising Day
"The longest word in the English language is the one following the phrase, 'And now a word from our sponsor.' "—*Hal Eaton (biographical information not available)*

"Advertising is the art of making whole lies out of half-truths."
—*Edgar A. Shoaff (biographical information not available)*

"For every credibility gap there is a gullibility fill."—*Richard Clopton (biographical information not available)*

"I think that I shall never see
A billboard lovely as a tree
Indeed unless the billboards fall
I'll never see a tree at all."—*Ogden Nash*

Advice given to attendees at a 1923 conference on advertising: "Appeal to reason in your advertising, and you appeal to four percent of the human race."

FEBRUARY 18

Wendell L(ewis) Willkie, *American lawyer, business executive, politician and writer, born Feb 18, 1892*
"A good catchword can obscure analysis for fifty years."

Len Deighton, *English journalist, novelist, writer and producer, born Feb 18, 1929*
"In Mexico an air conditioner is called a politician because it makes a lot of noise but doesn't work very well."

"Sam" (Samuel) Levine, *American businessman and bon vivant, born Feb 18, 1933*
"You certainly take a long time making your pointless."

"Women live longer than men because it's not polite to interrupt them when they're talking."

"Love is the child of illusion and the parent of disillusion."

"I only steal from the best."

John Travolta, *American actor, born Feb 18, 1954*
"A confirmed bachelor is a guy who believes in wine, women, and so long."

FEBRUARY 19

(Sir) Cedric Hardwicke, *English actor, born Feb 19, 1893*
"Hollywood may be thickly populated, but to me it's still a bewilderness."

Lee Marvin, *American actor, born Feb 19, 1924*
"Love is generally valued at its highest during two periods in life: during the days of courting and the days in court."

FEBRUARY 20

Hesketh Pearson, *English actor, director and biographer, born Feb 20, 1887*
"Misquotation is the pride and privilege of the learned."

Robert B. Altman, *American director, born Feb 20, 1925*
"Nobody has ever made a good movie. Someday, someone will make half a good one."

FEBRUARY 21

Sacha Guitry, *French playwright, actor, director and producer, born Feb 21, 1885*
"When a man steals your wife, there is no better revenge than to let him keep her."

W(ystan) H(ugh) Auden, *American poet, playwright and critic, born Feb 21, 1907*
"A professor is one who talks in someone else's sleep."

"Political history is far too criminal a subject to be a fit thing to teach children."

"No poet or novelist wishes he were the only one who ever lived, but most of them wish they were the only one alive, and quite a number fondly believe their wish has been granted."

"My face looks like a wedding cake that has been left out in the rain."

Erma Bombeck, *American columnist and writer, born Erma Louise Fiste, Feb 21, 1927*
"Housework can kill you if done right."

"The only reason I would take up jogging is so that I could hear heavy breathing again."

"I came from a family of pioneers. My mother invented guilt in 1936."

FEBRUARY 22

Engineers' Week week, Sunday thru Saturday including Feb 22
George Washington, *American surveyor, farmer, soldier and 1st US President, born Feb 22, 1732*

On Jul 4, 1848, the cornerstone of the Washington Monument was laid, but money for construction ran out 8 years later. Congress refused to appropriate more at the time, and the job wasn't finished until 1885. (First in war, first in peace, last in the hearts of his Congressmen?)

"Engineers know all the angles."—*Anon.*

Cynics have claimed there are only six basic plots.
Frankenstein and My Fair Lady are really the same story.

Arthur Schopenhauer, *German philosopher and writer, born Feb 22,*
1788
"To marry is to halve your rights and double your duties."

James Russell Lowell, *American poet, essayist, critic, editor and*
diplomat, born Feb 22, 1819
"No, never say nothin' without you're compelled tu.
An' then don't say nothin' thet you can be held tu."

FEBRUARY 23

Cynics' Day
"Idealism is what precedes experience; cynicism is what follows."
    —*David T. Wolf (biographical information not available)*

"The cynics are right nine times out of ten."—*H.L. Mencken*

Leslie Halliwell, *English film consultant, writer and critic, born*
Feb 23, 1929
"Cynics have claimed there are only six basic plots. *Frankenstein*
and *My Fair Lady* are really the same story."

FEBRUARY 24

Dog Lover's Day
"A dog is the only thing on earth that loves you more than you love yourself."—*Josh Billings*

"The more I know of men, the more I like my dogs."—*Anon.*

George (Augustus) Moore, *Irish novelist, poet, playwright and journalist, born Feb 24, 1852*
"Know him? I know him so well that I haven't spoken to him in ten years."—*Oscar Wilde about George Moore*

FEBRUARY 25

"Jim" (James Gilmore) Backus, *American actor, born Feb 25, 1913*
"Many a man owes his success to his first wife—and his second wife to his success."

Anthony Burgess, *English novelist and critic, born John Anthony Burgess Wilson, Feb 25, 1917*
"Laugh and the world laughs with you, snore and you sleep alone."

FEBRUARY 26

Victor(-Marie) Hugo, *French poet, novelist and playwright, born Feb 26, 1802*
Probably the shortest letters ever written were ones exchanged by Hugo and his publisher. Hugo's letter asked how they liked the manuscript for *Les Miserables:* "?" and the publisher responded: "!"

FEBRUARY 27

Henry Wadsworth Longfellow, *American poet, born Feb 27, 1807*
He was the first American poet to earn a living solely (or was it soully?) from the writing of verse.

Peter De Vries, *American novelist and editor, born Feb 27, 1910*
"Every novel should have a beginning, a muddle, and an end."

"I don't for the life of me understand why people keep insisting marriage is doomed. All five of mine worked out."

"When I can no longer bear to think of the victims of broken homes, I begin to think of the victims of intact ones."

"I love being a writer. What I can't stand is the paperwork."

"Everybody hates me because I'm so universally liked."

Lawrence (George) Durrell, *English poet and novelist, born Feb 27, 1912*

"Poem: what happens when an anxiety meets a technique."

Edward T. Butler, *American lawyer and jurist, born Feb 27, 1918*

"If I was in business, I wouldn't be."

FEBRUARY 28

Flirting Day

"A flirt is a woman who thinks it's every man for herself."—*Anon.*

"Middle age: when a man returns a wink with a blink."—*Anon.*

Michel (Eyquem) de Montaigne, *French essayist and philosopher, born Feb 28, 1533*

"Marriage is like a cage; one sees the birds outside desperate to get in, and those inside equally desperate to get out."

FEBRUARY 29

Bachelor's Day

"A bachelor is a man dedicated to life, liberty, and the happiness of pursuit."—*Anon.*

"One of the advantages of living alone is that you don't have to wake up in the arms of a loved one."—*Marion Smith (biographical information not available)*

"I never married because there was no need. I have three pets at home which answer the same purpose as a husband. I have a dog which growls every morning, a parrot which swears all the afternoon and a cat that comes home late at night."—*Marie Corelli, English novelist, born Mary Mackay, 1855 (birth date not available)*

"There is one woman whom fate has destined for each of us. If we miss her we are saved."—*Anon.*

"It is more blessed to give than to receive; for example, wedding presents."—*H.L. Mencken*

"Marriage isn't a word—it's a sentence."—*Anon.*

March

National Nutrition Month

National Nutrition Month

"Only Irish coffee provides in a single glass all four essential food groups: alcohol, caffeine, sugar, and fat."—*Alex Levine (biographical information not available)*

"With packaging materials in short supply people may have to eat fresh food."—*The Economist*

Poetry Month
In March 1740 Justice of the Peace Henry Fielding summoned
Poet Laureate Colley Cibber to court for the murder of the English
language.

"Poetry is the stuff in books that doesn't quite reach the
margins."—*Anonymous child*

"A poet can survive everything but a misprint."—*Anon.*

"Poets aren't very useful
Because they aren't consumeful or produceful."—*Ogden Nash*

"FLOATING" HOLIDAYS THIS MONTH

Save Your Vision Week first week, Sunday thru Saturday
"No one is ever so blind as not to be able to see another person's
duty."—*Anon.*

Men have better daylight vision than women; women have better
night vision. Be careful in the dark, fellas.

Procrastination Week first week, Monday thru Sunday
"Never put off until tomorrow what can be avoided altogether."
—*Anon.*

Art Week last week, Monday thru Sunday
"The misfortune of the 'artistic temperament' is that so many
people have the temperament and so few the art."—*J(ohn) Alfred
Spender, English journalist, editor and writer, born Dec 1862
(birth date not available)*

"The rarest thing in the world is a woman who is pleased with a
portrait of herself."—*Anon.*

"Only painters and lawyers can change white to black."—*Anon.*

Agriculture Day third Monday
"Two farmers each claimed to own a certain cow. While one pulled
on its head and the other on its tail, the cow was milked by a
lawyer."—*Jewish parable*

Vernal Equinox in Northern Hemisphere (Spring begins) about
Mar 21
"Spring: when boys begin to feel gallant and girls begin to feel
buoyant."—*Anon.*

"A little Madness in the Spring is wholesome even for the King."
—*Emily Dickinson*

MARCH 1

Return the Borrowed Books Week Mar 1-7
"All things come to those who wait except loaned books."—*Anon.*

Augustus Saint-Gaudens, *American sculptor, born Mar 1, 1848*
"What garlic is to salad, insanity is to art."

(James) David (Graham) Niven, *Scottish actor, born Mar 1, 1909*
On acting: "Can you imagine being wonderfully overpaid for dressing up and playing games?"

"Print anything you like, and I'll swear I said it."

"I once described my face as a cross between two pounds of halibut and an explosion in an old clothes closet."

Somers White, *American banker, consultant and politician, born Mar 1, 1931*
"Money can't buy friends, but you do get a better class of enemy."

Ron Howard, *American actor and director, born Mar 1, 1954*
"There's nothing wrong with teenagers that reasoning with them won't aggravate."

MARCH 2

Katharine (Elizabeth) Whitehorn, *English columnist and writer, born Mar 2, 1928*
"The main purpose of children's parties is to remind you that there are children more awful than your own."

"In my next life I would like to be a pessimist. And then other people could spend all their time cheering me up."

"A food is not necessarily essential just because your child hates it."

MARCH 3

Jean Harlow, *American actress, born Harlean Carpentier, Mar 3, 1911*
"The women like me because I don't look like a girl who would steal a husband. At least not for long."

"I like to wake up feeling a new man."

MARCH 4

William Targ, *American editor, publisher and writer, born William Torgownik, Mar 4, 1907*
"The trouble with the publishing business is that too many people who have half a mind to write a book do so."

Robert Orben, *American speechwriter and comedy writer, born Mar 4, 1927*

"Most people want to be delivered from temptation but would like it to keep in touch."

"I take my children everywhere, but they always find their way back home."

"If you want to walk the streets safely at night, carry a projector and slides from your last vacation."

"I could now afford all the things I never had as a kid, if I didn't have kids."

"To reduce stress, avoid excitement. Spend more time with your spouse."

"Every morning I get up and look through the Forbes list of the richest people in America. If I'm not there, I go to work."

MARCH 5

Andy Gibb, *English musician, born Mar 5, 1958*

"Girls are always running through my mind. They don't dare walk."

MARCH 6

Mind Your Manners Day

"Night clubs are places where the tables are reserved and the guests aren't."—*Frank Caspar, American radio comedian (birth date not available)*

"To succeed in life it is not enough to be stupid. One must be well mannered as well."—*Bonar Thompson, English actor, broadcaster, editor and writer, born 1888 (birth date not available)*

"Politeness is only one half good manners and the other half good lying."—*Mary Wilson Little (biographical information not available)*

Ring Lardner, *American journalist, short-story writer, playwright and humorist, born Ringgold Wilmer, Mar 6, 1885*

"I've known what it is to be hungry, but I always went right to a restaurant."

MARCH 7

Tell the Truth Day

"Old men and far travellers may lie by authority."—*Anon.*

"He who speaks the truth should have one foot in the stirrup."
    —*Hindi saying*

"Whoever tells the truth is chased out of nine villages."
    —*Turkish proverb*

"O what a tangled web we weave
When first we practise to deceive
But when we've practised quite a while
How vastly we improve our style."
    —*J.R. Pope (biographical information not available)*

Alessandro (Francesco Tomaso Antonio) Manzoni, *Italian poet and novelist, born Mar 7, 1785*
    "You must always explain things frankly and explicitly to your lawyer ... it is for him to embroil them afterwards."

MARCH 8

International Women's Day
    "Of all the wild beasts of land or sea, the wildest is woman."
    —*Menander, Greek poet and playwright*

"Woman's word is never done."—*Anon.*

"A woman should pick an age and stick to it."—*Anon.*

"A youthful figure is what you get when you ask a woman her age."—*Anon.*

"Aperte mala cum est mulier, tum demum est bona." (Latin) When a woman is openly bad she is then at her best.

"In years gone by, a woman's stead
Depended on her homemade bread.
Today instead of the bread she's baking
We treasure her for the dough she's making."—*Anon.*

"What makes women especially appealing is that the rest of us are men."—*Anon.*

"The fantasy of every Australian man is to have two women—one cleaning and the other dusting."—*Maureen Murphy (biographical information not available)*

In written Chinese, the symbol for "trouble" represents two women under one roof.

Simon Cameron, *American financier, politician and US Secretary of War, born Mar 8, 1799*
    "An honest politician is one who, when he is bought, will stay bought."

International Women's Day

"Gene" (Eugene Devlan) Fowler, *American novelist, journalist, playwright and biographer, born Mar 8, 1890*
"Writing is easy. All you do is stare at a blank sheet of paper until drops of blood form on your forehead."

MARCH 9

Ernest Bevin, *English statesman and labor leader, born Mar 9, 1881*
"He objected to ideas only when others had them."—*A.J.P. Taylor about Ernest Bevin*

To a subordinate: "Anything you make a mistake about, I will get you out of, and anything you do well, I will take credit for."

Vyacheslav Mikhaylovich Molotov, *Russian editor, statesman and diplomat, born Mar 9, 1890*
"My so-called Foreign Minister.... He can't even find foreign countries on the map, let alone deal with them."—*Joseph Stalin about Vyacheslav Molotov*

"Mickey" (Frank Morrison) Spillane, *American novelist, born*
Mar 9, 1918
"My speed depends on the state of my bank account."

MARCH 10

Operator's Day
Alexander Graham Bell transmitted the first telephone message (to the next room), Mar 10, 1876.

Alexander Graham Bell offered rights to his new talking machine to Western Union for $100,000. Western Union President William Orton turned him down, saying, "What use could this company make of an electrical toy?"

MARCH 11

(Sir James) Harold Wilson, *English economist, statesman and Prime Minister, born Mar 11, 1916*
"If Harold Wilson ever went to school without any boots it was merely because he was too big for them."—*Ivor Bulwer-Thomas about Harold Wilson*

"I know more about football than politics."

Bruce (Buchanan) Dexter, *American journalist, novelist, short-story writer and editor, born Mar 11, 1929*
"He's the kind of person who knows only two notes of the musical scale: *dough* and *me*."

"The great advantage of movies over life is that you always know how things are going to come out."

"A person who asks for fame and fortune isn't asking too much, but nine times out of ten he's asking the wrong person."

"True love is very simple: you promise what you don't have, ask for what you can't possibly get, and then agree to live happily ever after."

"At least half of the exercise I get every day comes from jumping to conclusions."

MARCH 12

Boycott Something Day
Charles Cunningham Boycott, *English farmer and estate agent, born Mar 12, 1832*
In 1880 tenants asked Boycott to reduce rents because of dire eco-

nomic conditions and poor potato harvests; Boycott responded by serving the tenants with eviction notices, and the tenants retaliated by refusing to have any dealings with him. Hence the word "boycott."

Philip Guedalla, *English lawyer, biographer, historian and essayist, born Mar 12, 1889*
"Biography, like big-game hunting, is one of the recognised forms of sport, and it is unfair as only sport can be."

(Joseph) Lane Kirkland, *American labor leader, born Mar 12, 1922*
"If hard work were such a wonderful thing, surely the rich would have kept it to themselves."

Andrew Young, *American clergyman, civil rights leader, politician and diplomat, born Mar 12, 1932*
"Nothing is illegal if a hundred businessmen decide to do it."

MARCH 13

Thinkers' Day
"Despite inflation, a penny is still a fair price for the thoughts of many people."—*Anon.*

"If you think you have the solution, the question was poorly phrased."—*Robert Gordon (biographical information not available)*

Science has discovered it is the lower part of the face that gives away one's thoughts, not the eyes. (This is especially true when one opens it.)

Paul Fix, *American actor, director, producer and screenwriter, born Paul Fix Morrison, Mar 13, 1902*
"The only reason some people get lost in thought is because it's unfamiliar territory."

Julius H(iram) Comroe (Jr.), *American educator, born Mar 13, 1911*
"Serendipity is looking in a haystack for a needle and discovering the farmer's daughter."

MARCH 14

Thomas R(iley) Marshall, *American lawyer, politician and 28th US Vice President, born Mar 14, 1854*
"Once there were two brothers. One ran away to sea, the other was elected vice-president, and nothing was ever heard of either of them again."

Albert Einstein, *American physicist, born Mar 14, 1879*
"When you sit with a nice girl for two hours, you think it's only a minute. But when you sit on a hot stove for a minute, you think it's two hours. That's relativity."

"Perfection of means and confusion of ends seem to characterize our age."

"It is a sad fact that Man does not live for pleasure alone."

"The hardest thing in the world to understand is the income tax."

"If I had only known, I would have been a locksmith."

MARCH 15

Ides of March
Latin lesson for the day: "Cogito ergo spud." (I think, therefore I yam.)

Norm Van Brocklin, *American football player and coach, born Mar 15, 1926*
"If I ever needed a brain transplant, I'd choose a sportswriter because I'd want a brain that had never been used."

MARCH 16

Scientists Day
"Scientists should be on tap but not on top."—*Winston Churchill*

"A drug is that substance which when injected into a rat will produce a scientific report."—*Anon.*

"I'll donate my body to science on one condition: they let me know the results."—*Eileen Mason*

Jerry Lewis, *American actor, comedian, producer and director, born Joseph Levitch, Mar 16, 1926*
"I appeal to children, who know I get paid for doing what they get slapped for."

MARCH 17

St. Patrick's Day
"The Irish really are lucky: all they have to kiss to get ahead is the Blarney Stone."—*Anon.*

"May your luck be like the capital of Ireland: always Dublin."—*Anon.*

Gloria Swanson, *American actress and businesswoman, born Gloria May Josephine Svensson, Mar 17, 1899*
"I've given my memoirs far more thought than any of my marriages. You can't divorce a book."

MARCH 18

John (Hoyer) Updike, *American novelist, poet and short-story writer, born Mar 18, 1932*
> "A healthy male bore consumes, each year, one and a half times his weight in other people's patience."

> "School is where you go between when your parents can't take you and industry can't take you."

> "Russia is the only country in the world you can be homesick for while you're still in it."

MARCH 19

"Max" (Johann Baptist Joseph Maximilian) Reger, *German composer, pianist and conductor, born Mar 19, 1873*
> "The life of a composer is work, hope, and bicarbonate of soda."

> "I am sitting in the smallest room in my house. I have your review in front of me. Soon it will be behind me."

Joseph (Warren) ("Vinegar Joe") Stilwell, *American army officer, born Mar 19, 1883*
> "The higher a monkey climbs, the more you see of its behind."

MARCH 20

Charles W(illiam) Eliot, *American educator and editor, born Mar 20, 1834*
> On being congratulated for making Harvard a storehouse of knowledge: "... I scarcely deserve the credit for that. It is simply that the freshmen bring so much knowledge in, and the seniors take so little out."

MARCH 21

Memory Day
> "Memory is the thing you forget with."—*Alexander Chase (biographical information not available)*

> "Of all the things I've ever lost, I miss my mind the most."—*Anon.*

> PATIENT: "I'm having trouble with my memory."
> DOCTOR: "When did this begin?"
> PATIENT: "When did what begin?"—*Anon.*

"There are three things I always forget: names, faces and—the third I can't remember."—*Anon.*

"Nostalgia is like a grammar lesson. You find the present tense and the past perfect."—*Anon.*

Eating after learning enhances memory in animals, including humans, because of the secretion by the stomach of CCK (cholecystokinin), a neurotransmitter associated with memory.

Teenager's Day

"Adolescence is the age at which children stop asking questions because they know all the answers."—*Anon.*

"The trouble with the 1980's as compared with the 1970's is that teenagers no longer rebel and leave home."—*Marion Smith (biographical information not available)*

"If you want to recapture your youth, just cut off his allowance."
—*Anon.*

MARCH 22

Goof-Off Day

"Loafing needs no explanation and is its own excuse."
—*Christopher Morley*

"The hardest work of all is to do nothing."—*Jewish proverb*

Hold Your Tongue Day

Marcel Marceau, *French actor, director and pantomimist, born Mar 22, 1923*

"Blessed is he who, having nothing to say, refrains from giving wordy evidence of the fact."—*Anon.*

"Whatever I said in anger,
whatever I shouted in spite,
I'm sorry I spoke so quickly—
I thought up some worse ones tonight."—*Sunshine Magazine*

"Many a man's tongue has broken his nose."—*Anon.*

"A man is known by the silence he keeps."—*Anon.*

"It is a good answer that knows when to stop."—*Anon.*

"Even four horses cannot pull back what the tongue has let go."
—*Slovakian saying*

"One of the best ways to persuade others is with your ears—
by listening to them."—*Anon.*

Maurice H(ubert) Stans, *American accountant, banker, politician, writer, government official and US Secretary of Commerce, born Mar 22, 1908*

"Good budgeting produces a uniform distribution of dissatisfaction."

Hold Your Tongue Day

MARCH 23

World Meteorological Day

"We regret we are unable to give you the weather. We rely on weather reports from the airport, which is closed because of the weather. Whether we are able to give you the weather tomorrow depends on the weather."—*Arab News*

"The climate of England has been the world's most powerful colonizing impulse."—*Russell Green, English writer, born 1893 (birth date not available)*

Putting ten people in a medium-sized room will raise the room's temperature one degree an hour. (Two people and their lawyers in court can raise it a degree a minute.)

Wernher (Magnus Maximilian) Von Braun, *American engineer and space scientist, born Mar 23, 1912*

"There is just one thing I can promise you about the outer-space program: Your tax dollar will go farther."

"We can lick gravity, but sometimes the paperwork is overwhelming."

"Basic research is what I am doing when I don't know what I am doing."

"Marty" (Martin) Allen, *American comedian, born Mar 23, 1922*
"A study of economics usually reveals that the best time to buy anything is last year."

MARCH 24

Malcolm (Thomas) Muggeridge, *English editor, journalist, broadcaster and writer, born Mar 24, 1903*
"It must be admitted that we English have sex on the brain, which is a very unfortunate place to have it."

"The world is so overflowing with absurdity that it is difficult for the humorist to compete."

Dwight MacDonald, *American journalist, editor, writer and critic, born Mar 24, 1906*
"A foundation is a large body of money completely surrounded by people who want some."

MARCH 25

Global Understanding Day
In 1929, Secretary of State Henry Stimson announced that the United States had no intention of recognizing the Government of the Soviet Union. Four years later full diplomatic relations were established.

"A chip on the shoulder indicates there is wood higher up."—*Anon.*

Howard Cosell, *American sportscaster, born Howard William Cohen, Mar 25, 1920*
"Arrogant, pompous, obnoxious, vain, cruel, persecuting, distasteful, verbose, a show-off. I have been called all of these. Of course, I am."

(Mary) Flannery O'Connor, *American novelist and short-story writer, born Mar 25, 1925*
"Everywhere I go I'm asked if I think the university stifles writers. My opinion is that they don't stifle enough of them. There's many a bestseller that could have been prevented by a good teacher."

Gloria Steinem, *American journalist, editor, writer and feminist, born Mar 25, 1934*
"Some of us are becoming the men we wanted to marry."

"Logic is in the eye of the logician."

"The reason most women don't gamble is that their total instinct for gambling is satisfied by marriage."

MARCH 26

Robert (Lee) Frost, *American poet, born Mar 26, 1874*

"The brain is a wonderful organ; it starts working the moment you get up in the morning and does not stop until you get to the office."

"A liberal is a man too broad-minded to take his own side in a quarrel."

"Education is the ability to listen to almost anything without losing your temper or your self-confidence."

"By working faithfully eight hours a day you may eventually get to be a boss and work twelve hours a day."

"A mother takes twenty years to make a man of her boy, and another woman makes a fool of him in twenty minutes."

"I've run more risk eating my way across the country than in all my driving."—Duncan Hines

"A bank is a place where they lend you an umbrella in fair weather and ask for it back when it begins to rain."

"Home is the place where,
when you have to go there,
They have to take you in."

"Never ask of money spent
Where the spender thinks it went.
Nobody was ever meant
To remember or invent
What he did with every cent."

"The world is full of willing people: some willing to work, the rest willing to let them."

"A jury consists of twelve persons chosen to decide who has the better lawyer."

"There is one thing more exasperating than a wife who can cook and won't, and that's the wife who can't cook and will."

"Education doesn't change life much. It just lifts trouble to a higher plane of regard."

Duncan Hines, *American culinary expert, writer and publisher, born Mar 26, 1880*

"I've run more risk eating my way across the country than in all my driving."

"Chico" (Leonard) Marx, *American actor and comedian, born Mar 26, 1886*

"I wasn't kissing her, I was whispering in her mouth."

Tennessee Williams, *American playwright, born Thomas Lanier Williams, Mar 26, 1911*

"We are all of us guinea-pigs in the laboratory of God. Humanity is just a work in progress."

"A vacuum is a hell of a lot better than some of the stuff that nature replaces it with."

MARCH 27

(Leonard) James Callaghan, *English politician and Prime Minister, born Mar 27, 1912*

"There is nobody in politics I can remember, and no case I can think of in history where a man combined such a powerful political personality with so little intelligence."—*Roy Jenkins about James Callaghan*

"A lie can be half way round the world before the truth has got its boots on."

Budd (Wilson) Schulberg, *American novelist, screenwriter and journalist, born Mar 27, 1914*
  "Living with a conscience is like driving a car with the brakes on."

MARCH 28

Realtors' Day
  "The first person to make a mountain out of a molehill was a real estate agent."—*Anon.*

Anthony (Meredith) Quinton, *English teacher, editor, translator, writer and critic, born Mar 28, 1925*
  "Architecture is the most inescapable of the higher arts."

MARCH 29

Eugene (Joseph) McCarthy, *American teacher, politician and writer, born Mar 29, 1916*
  "The only thing that saves us from the bureaucracy is its inefficiency."

  "Being in politics is like being a football coach. You have to be smart enough to understand the game and dumb enough to think it's important."

MARCH 30

Doctor's Day
  "My doctor's on the Golf Diet. He lives on greens."—*Anon.*

  "A specialist is a doctor whose patients are expected to confine their ailments to office hours."—*Anon.*

  "Doctor: A person who takes out a stethoscope and listens to your wallet."—*Anon.*

  "Some doctors make the same mistakes for twenty years and call it clinical experience."—*Anon.*

  During the New York doctors' strike of 1975, the death rate fell by more than fifteen percent.

Sean O'Casey, *Irish playwright, born John Casey, Mar 30, 1880*
  "We ought to have as great a regard for religion as we can, so as to keep it out of as many things as possible."

MARCH 31

Philosopher's Day

René Descartes, *French philosopher, scientist and mathematician ("father of modern philosophy"), born Mar 31, 1596*

"Psychiatry's chief contribution to philosophy is the discovery that the toilet is the seat of the soul."—*Alexander Chase (biographical information not available)*

"We can be absolutely certain only about things we do not understand."—*Anon.*

"I used to have all the answers; now I don't even know what the questions are."—*Eileen Mason*

Henry Morgan, *American actor and comedian, born Henry Lerner Von Ost, Jr., Mar 31, 1915*

"A kleptomaniac is a person who helps himself because he can't help himself."

John Fowles, *English novelist, born Mar 31, 1926*

"The old woman ... decided that even lawyers can be thieves—a possibility few who have had to meet their fees would dispute."

April

"April's the month when the green returns to the lawn, the lilac and the IRS."—Changing Times

Humor Month

"The gods too are fond of a joke."—*Aristotle, Greek philosopher*

"He who laughs, lasts."—*Mary Pettibone Poole (biographical information not available)*

A regular diet of laughter is as effective as biofeedback for controlling stress.

"FLOATING" HOLIDAYS THIS MONTH

Secretaries' Week last week, Sunday thru Saturday

Secretaries' Day Wednesday of Secretaries' Week
"Our secretaries have a perfect attendance record: they've never missed a coffee break."—*Anon.*

Consumer Protection Week fourth week, Monday thru Friday
"I know what I wish Ralph Nader would investigate next. Marriage... it's not safe at all."—*Jean Kerr*

Daylight Saving Time begins in United States first Sunday at 2 AM
Spring forward one hour.

APRIL 1

April Fool's Day
"April 1. This is the day upon which we are reminded of what we are on the other three hundred and sixty-four."—*Mark Twain*

"Never show a fool a half-finished job."—*Anon.*

"He who would make a fool of himself will find many to help him."—*Danish saying*

"Jim" (James) Fisk, *American financier, born Apr 1, 1834*
"There goes Jim Fisk, with his hands in his own pockets for a change."—*Anon*

Agnes Repplier, *American essayist, born Apr 1, 1855*
"Conversation between Adam and Eve must have been difficult at times because they had nobody to talk about."

APRIL 2

International Children's Book Day
Hans Christian Andersen, *Danish children's author, born Apr 2, 1805*

Frédéric-Auguste Bartholdi, *French sculptor (designer of US Statue of Liberty), born Apr 2, 1834*
"America is an adorable woman chewing tobacco."

Kurt Herbert Adler, *American conductor and opera director, born Apr 2, 1905*
"Tradition is what you resort to when you don't have the time or the money to do it right."

(Sir) Alec Guinness, *English actor, born Apr 2, 1914*
"I don't really know who I am. Quite possibly, I do not exist at all."

Kenneth (Peacock) Tynan, *English drama critic, playwright and theatrical executive, born Apr 2, 1927*
"A good many inconveniences attend play-going in any large city, but the greatest of them is usually the play itself."

Nomi Whalen, *Canadian family mediation therapist and political advisor, born Apr 2, 1932*
"Insanity: doing the same thing over and over and expecting a different result."

APRIL 3

Washington Irving, *American lawyer, short-story writer, essayist and writer, born Apr 3, 1783*
"A sharp tongue is the only edged tool that grows keener with constant use."

Herb (Eugene) Caen, *American columnist, born Apr 3, 1916*
"The trouble with Oakland is that when you get there, it's there."

"It is better to have loved and lost, but only if you have a good lawyer."

"Like a camel, I can go without a drink for seven days—and have on several horrible occasions."

Marlon Brando (Jr.), *American actor, born Apr 3, 1924*
"An actor's a guy who, if you ain't talking about him, ain't listening."

"The only reason I'm here is because I don't yet have the moral strength to turn down the money."

Doris Day, *American actress and singer, born Doris von Kappelhoff, Apr 3, 1924*
"Doris Day is as wholesome as a bowl of cornflakes and at least as sexy."—*Dwight MacDonald about Doris Day*

"It's my cameraman who is getting older."

APRIL 4

Bankers' Day
"The person who writes the bank's commercials is not the person who makes the loans."—*Anon.*

"Bankers have a lot of horse sense—they've a lot of practice saying 'Neigh.' "—*Anon.*

APRIL 5

Spencer Tracy, *American actor, born Apr 5, 1900*
Asked what he looks for in a script: "Days off."

"Acting is not an important job in the scheme of things. Plumbing is."

Bette Davis, *American actress, born Ruth Elizabeth Davis, Apr 5, 1908*
"Nobody's as good as Bette when she's bad."—*said in Hollywood about Bette Davis*

"Old age is no place for sissies."

"Old age—that's the period of life when you buy yourself a see-through nightgown and then remember you don't know anybody who can still see through one!"

"Some young Hollywood starlets remind me of my grandmother's old farmhouse—all painted up nice on the front side, a big swing on the backside, and nothing whatsoever in the attic."

APRIL 6

Wife's Day
Brigham Young, Mormon Church leader, married his 27th (and last) wife Apr 6, 1868.

"Bigamy is having one wife too many. Monogamy is the same thing."—*Anon.*

"Marriage: When a man agrees to give a woman the best ears of his life."—*Anon.*

"By all means marry. If you get a good wife, you will become happy; and if you get a bad one, you will become a philosopher."
    —*Socrates, Greek philosopher*

"A bigamist is a man who marries a beautiful woman and a good cook."—*Anon.*

"In the old days, men rode chargers. Now they marry them."—*Anon.*

"Whether you end up with a nest egg or a goose egg depends on the kind of chick you married."—*Wall Street Journal*

"I am feeling very lonely. I've been married for fifteen years, and yesterday my wife ran off with the chap next door. I'm going to miss him terribly."—*Les Dawson, English writer (birth date not available)*

APRIL 7

World Health Day
World Health Organization established April 7, 1948.

Walter Winchell, *American gossip columnist and broadcaster, born Walter Winchel, Apr 7, 1897*

"Gossip is the art of saying nothing in a way that leaves practically nothing unsaid."

Hollywood: "A place where they shoot too many pictures and not enough actors."

"Hollywood is a place where they place you under contract instead of under observation."

Optimist: "a man who gets treed by a lion but enjoys the scenery."

Billie Holiday, *American singer, born Eleanora Fagan, Apr 7, 1915*

"Mom and Pop were just a couple of kids when they got married. He was eighteen, she was sixteen, and I was three."

"Jerry" (Edmund Gerald) Brown (Jr.), *American lawyer and politician, born Apr 7, 1938*

"I see the world in very fluid, contradictory, emerging, inter-connected terms, and with that kind of circuitry I just don't feel the need to say what is going to happen or will not happen."

David (Parradine) Frost, *English television host, producer, performer and writer, born Apr 7, 1939*

"He rose without trace."—*Kitty Muggeridge about David Frost*

"Television enables you to be entertained in your home by people you wouldn't have in your home."

APRIL 8

E(dgar) Y(ipsel) Harburg, *American lyricist, born Apr 8, 1896*

"Virtue is its own revenge."

Sonja Henie, *Norwegian skater and actress, born Apr 8, 1912*

"Jewellery takes people's minds off your wrinkles."

APRIL 9

Charles(-Pierre) Baudelaire, *French poet, translator and critic, born Apr 9, 1821*

"What is irritating about love is that it is a crime that requires an accomplice."

"It is by universal misunderstanding that all agree. For if, by ill luck, people understood each other, they would never agree."

Jean-Paul Belmondo, *French actor, born Apr 9, 1933*

"Women over thirty are at their best, but men over thirty are too old to recognize it."

APRIL 10

William Booth, *English religious leader (founder of Salvation Army), born Apr 10, 1829*

"If Moses had operated through committees the Israelites never would have got across the Red Sea."

Clare Boothe Luce, *American journalist, playwright, politician and diplomat, born Apr 10, 1903*

When told that Luce was invariably kind to her inferiors: "Where does she find them?"—*Dorothy Parker about Clare Booth Luce*

"A man's home may seem to be his castle on the outside; inside, it is more often his nursery."

"The politicians were talking themselves red, white and blue in the face."

"Whenever a Republican leaves one side of the aisle and goes to the other [Democratic], it raises the intelligence quotient of both parties."

"If Moses had operated through committees the Israelites never would have got across the Red Sea."

"I don't have a warm personal enemy left. They've all died off. I miss them terribly because they helped define me."

Marvin Bressler, *American teacher and writer, born Apr 10, 1923*
"There is no crisis to which academics will not respond with a seminar."

Omar Sharif, *Egyptian actor and bridge expert, born Michael Shalhoub, Apr 10, 1932*
"The only premarital thing girls don't do these days is cooking."

APRIL 11

Dean (Gooderham) Acheson, *American lawyer, statesman and US Secretary of State, born Apr 11, 1893*
"Time spent in the advertising business seems to create a permanent deformity like the Chinese habit of foot-binding."

Asked of his plans when he left his post as Secretary of State: "I will undoubtedly have to seek what is happily known as gainful employment, which I am glad to say does not describe holding public office."

APRIL 12

(Francis) Claud Cockburn, *English journalist, editor and writer, born Apr 12, 1904*
"Never believe anything until it has been officially denied."

George Velliotes, *American teacher and political satirist, born Apr 12, 1928*
"One person is a human being; two people is politics."

David Letterman, *American television host and comedian, born Apr 12, 1947*
"Sometimes when you look in his eyes you get the feeling that someone else is driving."

APRIL 13

Thomas Jefferson, *American lawyer, educator, architect, politician and 3rd US President, born Apr 13, 1743*
"Advertisements contain the only truths to be relied on in a newspaper."

"I do not take a single newspaper, nor read one a month, and I feel myself infinitely the happier for it."

Samuel (Barclay) Beckett, *Irish novelist, playwright and critic, born Apr 13, 1906*
"We are all born mad, and some remain so."

APRIL 14

James Branch Cabell, *American novelist, journalist, editor and essayist, born Apr 14, 1879*
"The optimist proclaims that we live in the best of all possible worlds, and the pessimist fears this is true."

Arnold (Joseph) Toynbee, *English historian, born Apr 14, 1889*
"America is a large friendly dog in a small room. Every time it wags its tail it knocks over a chair."

"Pete" (Peter Edward) Rose, *American baseball player and manager, born Apr 14, 1942*
"Women are a lot like umpires. They make quick decisions, never reverse them, and they don't think you're safe when you're out."

"I'm no different from anybody else with two arms, two legs, and forty-two hundred hits."

APRIL 15

Uncle Sam's Pay-Day Tax returns due in United States
"The IRS believes the United States is a land of untold wealth."
—*Anon.*

"No longer does 1040 scare me;
I fill it without any sufferin'.
I read the instructions,
Grab hold of my pen,
And my aspirin, my Anacin
And my Bufferin."—*Anon.*

"Today it takes more brains and effort to make out the income-tax form than it does to make the income."—*Alfred E. Neuman (biographical information not available)*

"Next to being shot at and missed, nothing is really quite as satisfying as an income tax refund."—*F.J. Raymond (biographical information not available)*

"It is getting harder and harder to support the government in the style to which it has become accustomed."—*Anon.*

"To err is human
But this you should learn
Don't be human on your tax return."—*Anon.*

Henry James, *English novelist, born Apr 15, 1843*
"A mind so fine that no idea could violate it."—*T.S. Eliot about Henry James*

"Henry James was one of the nicest old ladies I ever met."
—*William Faulkner about Henry James*

(Lord) John Edward Poynder Grigg Altrincham, *English journalist, editor and writer, born Apr 15, 1924*
> "Autobiography is now as common as adultery and hardly less reprehensible."

APRIL 16

Anatole France, *French novelist and critic, born Jacques-Anatole-François Thibault, Apr 16, 1844*
> "Without lies humanity would perish of despair and boredom."

> "It is better to understand a little than to misunderstand a lot."

"Charlie" (Sir Charles Spencer) Chaplin, *English actor and director, born Apr 16, 1889*
> "In the end, everything is a gag."

> "There are more valid facts and details in works of art than there are in history books."

> "Age has its compensations. It is less apt to be brow-beaten by discretion."

> "I remain one thing and one thing only, and that is a clown. It places me on a far higher plane than any politician."

Peter (Alexander) Ustinov, *English actor, producer, director, playwright, screenwriter and novelist, born Apr 16, 1921*
> "Parents are the bones on which children sharpen their teeth."

> "British education is probably the best in the world, if you can survive it. If you can't there is nothing left for you but the diplomatic corps."

Kingsley Amis, *English novelist and poet, born Apr 16, 1922*
> "It is no wonder that people are so horrible when they start life as children."

> "If you can't annoy somebody, there is little point in writing."

> "He was of the faith chiefly in the sense that the church he currently did not attend was Catholic."

APRIL 17

Nikita (Sergeyevich) Khrushchev, *Russian politician and Soviet Premier, born Apr 17, 1894*
> "Politicians are the same everywhere. They promise to build bridges even where there are no rivers."

"When you are skinning your customers you should leave some skin on to grow, so that you can skin them again."

Thornton (Niven) Wilder, *American playwright and novelist, born Apr 17, 1897*

"Marriage is a bribe to make a housekeeper think she's a house-holder."

"We'll trot down to the movies and see how girls with wax faces live."

"The best thing about animals is that they don't talk much."

"It's your combination sinners—your lecherous liars and your miserly drunkards—who dishonor the vices and bring them into disrepute."

William Holden, *American actor, born William Beedle, Apr 17, 1918*

"I found the greatest sleeping pill in the world: this script."

"Tom" (Thomas Joseph) Glassic, *American football player and entrepreneur, born Apr 17, 1954*

"Did you know they're making TV dinners a lot better now than they used to? It'll help some guys decide to stay single."

APRIL 18

Clarence (Seward) Darrow, *American lawyer, novelist and writer, born Apr 18, 1857*

"The first half of our lives is ruined by our parents and the second half by our children."

"When I was a boy I was told that anybody could become President; I'm beginning to believe it."

"I have never killed a man, but I have read many obituaries with a lot of pleasure."

Richard Harding Davis, *American journalist, novelist and play-wright, born Apr 18, 1864*

"No civilized person ever goes to bed the same day he gets up."

APRIL 19

Jayne Mansfield, *American actress, born Vera Jane Palmer, Apr 19, 1932*

"Men are those creatures with two legs and eight hands."

Dudley (Stuart John) Moore, *English actor, composer and pianist, born Apr 19, 1935*

"I'm always looking for meaningful one-night stands."

APRIL 20

Andrew (Previn) Tobias, *American columnist and writer, born Apr 20, 1947*
"You can live well if you're rich and you can live well if you're poor, but if you're poor, it's much cheaper."

APRIL 21

Josh Billings, *American humorist, born Henry Wheeler Shaw, Apr 21, 1818*
"To enjoy a good reputation, give publicly and steal privately."

"The trouble with people is not that they don't know, but that they know so much that ain't so."

"As scarce as truth is, the supply has always been in excess of the demand."

"There's lots of people in this world who spend so much time watching their health that they haven't the time to enjoy it."

"Always live within your income, even if you have to borrow money to do so."

"I don't care how much a man talks, if he only says it in a few words."

Oscar (Lewis) Wright, *American teacher and Small Business Advocate in California, born Apr 21, 1917*
Advice to small business owners in California: "If you feel you're still going to have a nervous breakdown, come on up to Sacramento where it won't be noticed."

APRIL 22

Cat Lovers' Day
"He who doesn't like the cat
Must have one time been a rat."—*Anon.*

Henry Fielding, *English novelist and playwright, born Apr 22, 1707*
"His designs were strictly honourable, as the saying is; that is, to rob a lady of her fortune by way of marriage."

APRIL 23

William Shakespeare, *English poet and playwright, born Apr 23, 1564*
"Though I am not naturally honest, I am so sometimes by chance."

**"He who doesn't like the cat
Must have one time been a rat."**

Shirley Temple Black, *American actress and diplomat, born
Apr 23, 1928*
   "I class myself with Rin Tin Tin. People were looking for something
   to cheer them up. They fell in love with a dog and a little girl."

APRIL 24

Anthony Trollope, *English novelist, born Apr 24, 1815*
   "He is the dullest Briton of them all."—*Henry James about Anthony
   Trollope*

(Sir Richard) Stafford Cripps, *English lawyer and statesman, born
Apr 24, 1889*
   "He has a brilliant mind, until he makes it up."—*Margot Asquith
   about Stafford Cripps*

   "There, but for the grace of God, goes God."—*Winston Churchill
   about Stafford Cripps*

Robert Penn Warren, *American teacher, poet, novelist and critic (first US Poet Laureate), born Apr 24, 1905*
"Poets are terribly sensitive people and one of the things they are most sensitive about is cash."

Shirley MacLaine, *American actress and writer, born Shirley Beatty, Apr 24, 1934*
"It's useless to hold a person to anything he says while he's in love, drunk, or running for office."

Barbra Streisand, *American singer and actress, born Barbara Joan Streisand, Apr 24, 1942*
"You think beautiful girls are going to stay in style forever?"

APRIL 25

Walter (John) de la Mare, *English novelist, poet and anthologist, born Apr 25, 1873*
"It's a very odd thing—
As odd as can be—
That whatever Miss T. eats
Turns into Miss T."

Edward R. Murrow, *American journalist, newscaster and director of US Information Agency, born Egbert Roscoe Murrow, Apr 25, 1908*
"Just because your voice reaches halfway around the world doesn't mean you are wiser than when it reached only to the end of the bar."

"Al" (Alfred) Pacino, *American actor, born Apr 25, 1940*
"I don't need any bodyguards. I'm from the South Bronx."

APRIL 26

(Ferdinand-Victor-)Eugène Delacroix, *French painter, born Apr 26, 1798*
"Men will always prefer toys to objects worthy of their admiration."

Artemus Ward, *American journalist and humorist, born Charles Farrar Browne, Apr 26, 1834*
"Thrice is he armed that hath his quarrel just—and four times he who gets his fist in fust."

"I'm not a politician and my other habits are good."

Anita Loos, *American novelist and screenwriter, born Apr 26, 1893*
"Kissing your hand may make you feel very good, but a diamond bracelet lasts for ever."

"It isn't that gentlemen really prefer blondes, it's just that we look dumber."

Carol Burnett, *American comedienne, actress and singer, born Apr 26, 1933*
> "The first time someone said, 'What are your measurements?' I answered, 'Thirty-seven, twenty-four, thirty-eight—but not necessarily in that order.'"

APRIL 27

Musicians' Day
> "It has been reported that rock music is dying. There is no other way to account for the weird noise it makes."—*Anon.*

> "Old musicians never quit; they just decompose."—*Anon.*

Deciding that *The Sound of Music* was too long, a theater manager in South Korea shortened the film by cutting out all the songs.

APRIL 28

Karl Kraus, *Austrian essayist, poet and critic, born Apr 28, 1874*
> "Psychoanalysis is that mental illness for which it regards itself a therapy."

> "The making of a journalist: no ideas and the ability to express them."

Lionel Barrymore, *American actor, born Apr 28, 1878*
> "Well, I've played everything but a harp."

APRIL 29

J(ules) H(enri) Poincaré, *French mathematician, teacher and writer, born Apr 29, 1854*
> "Sociology is the science with the greatest number of methods and the least results."

(Sir) Thomas Beecham, *English conductor, born Apr 29, 1879*
> "A musicologist is a person who can read music but can't hear it."

> "There are only two things requisite so far as the public is concerned for a good performance. That is for the orchestra to begin together and end together. In between it doesn't matter much."

> "Three quarters of television is for half-wits."

> "The trouble with women in an orchestra is that if they are attractive it will upset my players and if they're not it will upset me."

> "On the whole I would prefer to conduct for people in deepest Africa who beat tom-toms and live on nuts."

Rudy Joe Mano, *American manufacturing manager and sports official, born Apr 29, 1915*
"Whenever I run into somebody with their glasses resting on top of their head, I get the feeling they are getting ready to go to the moon. Or they just got back."

Celeste Holm, *American actress, born Apr 29, 1919*
"Acting is controlled schizophrenia."

APRIL 30

Husbands' Day
"Husbands should be like Kleenex: soft, strong, and disposable."
—*Clue (the movie)*

"A husband should tell his wife everything that he is sure she will find out."—*Thomas R. Dewar (biographical information not available)*

"A husband is one who stands by a woman in all the troubles she wouldn't have had if she hadn't married him."—*Anon.*

"All the women moaning about finding husbands have obviously never had one."—*Anon.*

"One good husband is worth two good wives, for the scarcer things are, the more they are valued."—*Benjamin Franklin*

May

Better Sleep Month

Older Americans Month

"*Si jeunesse savait, si vieillesse pouvait*" *(French saying).* If the young only knew; if the old only could.

"Experience is the comb life brings you after you have lost your hair."—*Judith Stern (biographical information not available)*

"A man could retire nicely in his old age if he could dispose of his experience for what it cost him."—*Anon.*

Mental Health Month

"Insanity: grounds for divorce in some states, grounds for marriage in all."—*Anon.*

"Psychiatry is the care of the id by the odd."—*Anon.*

"Neurotics build castles in the air. Psychotics live in them. Psychologists collect the rent."—*Anon.*

"The difference between a conjuror and a psychologist is that one pulls rabbits out of a hat and the other pulls habits out of a rat."
—*Anon.*

"Roses are red
Violets are blue
I'm schizophrenic
And so am I."—*Anon.*

"Schizophrenia beats dining alone."—Anon.

Physical Fitness Month

"One good thing about being in rotten physical shape—at least you don't have to exercise to keep it up."—*Anon.*

"You've reached middle age when all you exercise is caution."
—*Anon.*

"One would think the rat race would be exercise enough."—*Anon.*

"The important question is how long you should go without exercise before eating."—*Miss Piggy, Muppet actress*

"FLOATING" HOLIDAYS THIS MONTH

Be Kind to Animals Week first week, Sunday thru Saturday
"None of my patients are hypochondriacs but you should see some of the owners."—*Anonymous veterinary surgeon*

"Zoo: a place devised for animals to study the habits of human beings."—*Anon.*

World Trade Week third week, Sunday thru Saturday
"The Japanese have a real yen for American dollars."
—*Eileen Mason*

At a 1982 Confederation of British Industry Conference on the threat of foreign car imports, alert reporters counted in the parking lot a total of seventeen Mercedes, Citroen, Alfa Romeo, and BMW autos.

Transportation Week the week, Sunday thru Saturday, including the third Friday
"Traffic is very heavy at the moment, so if you are thinking of

leaving now, you'd better set off a few minutes earlier."—*Broadcaster for Automobile Association in London*

"What is it that disappears when you make a U-turn? A parking space."—*Anon.*

"He who hesitates is not only lost, but miles from the next exit."
—*Anon.*

"Please drive carefully. The IRS needs you."—*Anon.*

Mother's Day second Sunday
"Working mothers have it all ... a family, a career, a headache."—*Anon.*

Native American Day second Saturday
Message received by Vice President Lyndon Johnson from an American Indian: "Be careful with your immigration laws. We were careless with ours."

Armed Forces Day observed in United States third Saturday
"Military intelligence is a contradiction in terms."—*Groucho Marx*

"I once knew a woman who reminded me of the Marine Corps—she was looking for a few good men."—*Anon.*

"Soldiers are often AWOL (after women or liquor)."—*Anon.*

"The navy wears white so they're always ready to surrender."
—*Anonymous army lover*

Memorial Day observed in United States the last Monday

MAY 1

Loyalty Day

Joseph Addison, *English playwright, essayist, poet, critic and statesman, born May 1, 1672*
"We are always doing something for Posterity, but I would fain see Posterity do something for us."

Glenn Ford, *American actor, born Gwyllyn Ford, May 1, 1916*
"If they try to rush me, I always say, 'I've only got one other speed, and it's slower.'"

Joseph Heller, *American novelist, born May 1, 1923*
"Some men are born mediocre, some men achieve mediocrity, and some men have mediocrity thrust upon them."

"He was a self-made man who owed his lack of success to nobody."

"She was a crazy mathematics major from the Wharton School of Business who could not count to twenty-eight each month without getting into trouble."

"I'd like to see the government get out of war altogether and leave the whole field to private industry."

"I couldn't see much point in tying myself down to a middle-aged woman with four children, even though the woman was my wife and the children were my own."

MAY 2

Jerome K(lapka) Jerome, *English novelist and playwright, born May 2, 1859*
"I like work; it fascinates me. I can sit and look at it for hours."

Hedda Hopper, *American gossip columnist, born Elda Furry, May 2, 1890*
"For the first time in my life I envied my feet—they were asleep."

"Her singing was mutiny on the high C's."

Bernard Slade, *Canadian playwright, born Bernard Slade Newbound, May 2, 1930*
"A laugh is the reverse of a breakdown; it's a break up."

MAY 3

Niccolo Machiavelli, *Italian statesman, philosopher and writer, born May 3, 1469*
"It is better to be adventurous than cautious, because fortune is a woman."

Mary Astor, *American actress and novelist, born Lucile V. Langehanke, May 3, 1906*
"I was neither a peacock nor the girl next door, and heads turning in my direction always gave me sweaty palms."

Pete Seeger, *American singer and composer, born May 3, 1919*
"Education is when you read the fine print. Experience is what you get if you don't."

Mell Lazarus, *American cartoonist, novelist, playwright and humorist, born May 3, 1927*
"The secret of life is to skip having children and go directly to grandchildren."—*Momma, character created by Mell Lazarus*

MAY 4

Dreamers' Day
"If a man could have half his wishes, he would double his troubles."—*Anon.*

Warm-blooded animals dream, but cold-blooded ones do not, we're told. And animals (like human babies) requiring care by parents after birth dream less in the womb and more after birth than animals (like calves) which can take care of themselves right away. (Maybe because they're trying to figure out how they ended up in this predicament?)

MAY 5

Cinco de Mayo
Mexican troops, outnumbered 3 to 1, defeated French invaders at Battle of Puebla, May 5, 1862.

Sören (Aabye) Kierkegaard, *Danish philosopher and theologian, born May 5, 1813*
"If you marry, you will regret it. If you do not marry, you will also regret it."

Karl (Heinrich) Marx, *German sociologist, economist and philosopher, born May 5, 1818*
"Philosophy is to the real world as masturbation is to sex."

Christopher (Darlington) Morley, *American journalist, editor and novelist, born May 5, 1890*
"A human being: an ingenious assembly of portable plumbing."

"My theology, briefly, is that the universe was dictated, but not signed."

Tyrone (Edmund) Power, *American actor, born May 5, 1914*
"I've done an awful lot of stuff that's a monument to public patience."

MAY 6

Nurse's Day
An English hospital sent letters to its student nurses congratulating them on passing their exams, and telling them that they were fired because there were no permanent jobs to offer them. Had they failed their exams, they could have stayed on the job for another six months to prepare to retake them.

Sigmund Freud, *Austrian neurologist (founder of psychoanalysis), born May 6, 1856*
"The first human being who hurled an insult instead of a stone was the founder of civilization."

"Two can live as cheaply as one—if they both have good jobs."

"The great question ... which I have not been able to answer, despite my thirty years of research into the feminine soul, is, 'What does a woman want?' "

Rudolph Valentino, *American actor, born Rodolpho Alfonzo Rafaello Pietro Filiberto Guglieimi Di Valentina D'Antonguolla, May 6, 1895*
"He had the acting talents of the average wardrobe."—*Clyde Jeavons and Jeremy Pascall about Rudolph Valentino*

"To generalize on women is dangerous. To specialize on them is infinitely worse."

"We cannot know woman because she does not know herself."

"I am beginning to look more and more like my miserable imitators."

Randall Jarrell, *American poet, novelist and critic, born May 6, 1914*
"The people who live in a Golden Age usually go around complaining how yellow everything looks."

(George) Orson Welles, *American actor, producer, director and writer, born May 6, 1915*
"The law and the stage—both are a form of exhibitionism."

"A movie studio is the best toy a boy ever had."

"I began at the top and I've been working my way down ever since."

MAY 7

Robert Browning, *English poet, born May 7, 1812*
"He floods acres of paper with brackets and inverted commas."
—*Robert Louis Stevenson about Robert Browning*

"Well, I hope they understand one another—nobody else would."
—*William Wordsworth about the marriage in 1846 of Elizabeth Barrett and Robert Browning*

"Johnny" (John Constantine) Unitas, *American football player and restaurateur, born May 7, 1933*
"I could have played two or three more years. All I needed was a leg transplant."

MAY 8

Edward Gibbon, *English historian, born May 8, 1737*
"Unprovided with original learning, unformed in the habits of thinking, unskilled in the arts of composition, I resolved to write a book."

Harry S. Truman, *American farmer, judge, politician and 33rd US President, born May 8, 1884*
"The best way to give advice to your children is to find out what they want and then advise them to do it."

*"I could have played two or three more years. All I
needed was a leg transplant."*

"A statesman is a politician who has been dead ten or fifteen years."

"Men often mistake notoriety for fame and would rather be remembered for their vices and follies than not be noticed at all."

"It's a recession when your neighbor loses his job; it's a depression when you lose your own."

(Bishop) Fulton J(ohn) Sheen, *American clergyman, writer and broadcast personality, born Peter John Sheen, May 8, 1895*
"Every child should have an occasional pat on the back, as long as it is applied low enough, and hard enough.

MAY 9

(Sir) James M(atthew) Barrie, *Scottish playwright and novelist, born May 9, 1860*
"I know not, sir, whether Bacon wrote the works of Shakespeare, but if he did not it seems to me that he missed the opportunity of his life."

"I am not young enough to know everything."

Barbara (Blackburn) Woodhouse, *English animal trainer, born May 9, 1910*
> "I can train any dog in five minutes. It's training the owner that takes longer."

Albert Finney, *English actor, born May 9, 1936*
> "Now that I can afford all the shirts I want, I find people in shops insist I have them as a present."

"Billy" (William Martin) Joel, *American singer and songwriter, born May 9, 1949*
> "I don't look any better than I did ten years ago. How come all these girls are coming on to me now? Where were they in high school when I needed them?"

MAY 10

Fred Astaire, *American dancer and actor, born Frederick Austerlitz, May 10, 1899*
> "He is the nearest we are ever likely to get to a human Mickey Mouse."—*Graham Greene about Fred Astaire*

> "It was the kind of flop that made even the audience look bad."

J(ohn) D(esmond) Bernal, *Irish physicist, teacher and writer, born May 10, 1901*
> "The full area of ignorance is not yet mapped. We are at present only exploring its fringes."

MAY 11

Salvador (Felipe Jacinto) Dali, *Spanish artist, born May 11, 1904*
> "Bugs Bunny is the most ugly and frightening animal in the world. I will paint it with mayonnaise and make it an object of art."

Phil Silvers, *American comedian and actor, born Philip Silversmith, May 11, 1912*
> "It took him twenty years to become an overnight sensation."
> —*Milton Berle about Phil Silvers*

> "I've never won an interview yet."

"Mort" (Morton Lyon) Sahl, *Canadian comedian, born May 11, 1927*
> "Liberals feel unworthy of their possessions. Conservatives feel they deserve everything they've stolen."

> On himself: "Only in show business could a guy with a C-minus average be considered an intellectual."

MAY 12

Limerick Day

> "There was a young writer named Pyle
> Who penned verse in libidinous style;
> Asked why he wrote trash,
> He said, 'It's not the cash—
> I do it to make people smile.' "—*Anon.*

Hospital Day

Florence Nightingale, *English nurse and hospital administrator, born May 12, 1820*

Returning from the Crimean War at the age of 36, she was convinced she had a terminal disease and that her life hung by a thread. She lived her next 54 years as a semi-invalid, only dying at the age of 90.

Edward Lear, *English artist and poet, born May 12, 1812*

> "How pleasant to know Mr. Lear!
> Who has written such volumes of stuff!
> Some think him ill-tempered and queer,
> But a few think him pleasant enough."

"Yogi" (Lawrence Peter) Berra, *American baseball player, coach and manager, born May 12, 1925*

> "If people don't want to come out to the ball park, nobody's going to stop them."

MAY 13

Civil Servants' Day

> "The perfect civil servant is the man who has a valid objection to any possible solution."—*A.H. Keates (biographical information not available)*

> "A taxpayer is someone who does not have to pass a civil service exam to work for the government."—*Anon.*

> "Government is an institution through which sound travels faster than light."—*Anon.*

> "There's no trick to being a humorist when you have the whole government working for you."—*Will Rogers*

(Sir) Arthur S(eymour) Sullivan, *English composer and conductor, born May 13, 1842*

> "The theater is not a place for a musician. When the curtain is up the music interrupts the actor, and when it is down the music interrupts the audience."

MAY 14

Admit a Mistake Day

"People will listen a great deal more patiently while you explain your mistakes than when you explain your successes."—*Anon.*

"Experience teaches you to recognize a mistake when you've made it again."—*Anon.*

"A mistake at least proves somebody stopped talking long enough to do something."—*Anon.*

"He is always right who suspects that he makes mistakes."
—*Spanish saying*

In 1884, French officials reopened the case of Paul Hubert, who by then had served 21 years of a life sentence, because they finally realized he had been convicted of murdering himself.

A leaflet distributed by the Jobs Not Bombs youth marchers at an English Labour Party conference, said: "If the power of the Labour Party and trade unionists is fully mobilized then nuclear disarmament can be stopped."

Sign in an English fast food store: "Open seven days a week, Excluding Sundays."

After sending out about half a million singing telegrams and telephone messages to the tune of *Happy Birthday to You*, Western Union discovered the ditty had been copyrighted back in 1893 by Mildred and Patty Hill, who wrote it for schoolrooms as *Good Morning to All*.

Toast: "May the mistakes in our futures be infinitesimal compared to those in our pasts."—*Eileen Mason*

MAY 15

Richard J(oseph) Daley, *American politician, born May 15, 1902*
"The police are here not to create disorder. They are here to preserve disorder."

Joseph Cotten, *American actor, born May 15, 1905*
"... but, in the end, all we hope to reach is a high standard of compromise."

James Mason, *English actor, born May 15, 1909*
"I think the question people should ask is, 'Of all your films, which is the one you'd like most to have destroyed?' "

Max (Rudolf) Frisch, *Swiss architect, playwright and novelist, born May 15, 1911*

Admit a Mistake Day

"Technology is a way of organizing the universe so that man doesn't have to experience it."

MAY 16

Biographers' Day
On May 16, 1763 James Boswell and Samuel Johnson met for the first time in the back room of a London bookstore. Boswell said, "I do indeed come from Scotland, but I cannot help it."

"Anybody who profits from the experience of others probably writes biographies."—*Franklin P. Jones, American attorney, born 1906 (birth date not available)*

Henry (Jaynes) Fonda, *American actor, born May 16, 1905*
"My son got his first acting part, playing a man who's been married for thirty years. I told him to stick at it and next time he'd get a speaking part."

George Morris Lichty, *American cartoonist, born May 16, 1905*
"Politics is the art of compromise, boys.... You scratch my back, and I stab yours."—*Senator Snort, character created by George Morris Lichty*

(Wladziu Valentino) Liberace, *American pianist and entertainer, born May 16, 1919*
To the critics: "What you said hurt me very much. I cried all the way to the bank."

"My age is 39 plus tax."

MAY 17

Stockbroker's Day
New York Stock Exchange founded May 17, 1792.

"A broker is a man who runs your fortune into a shoestring."
—*Alexander Woollcott*

"With an evening coat and a white tie, anybody, even a stockbroker, can gain a reputation for being civilized."—*Oscar Wilde*

Erik(-Alfred-Leslie) Satie, *French composer, born May 17, 1866*
"The musician is perhaps the most modest of animals, but he is also the proudest. It is he who invented the sublime art of ruining poetry."

Clark Kerr, *American economist and educator, born May 17, 1911*
"A university anywhere can aim no higher than to be as British as possible for the sake of the undergraduates, as German as possible for the sake of the public at large—and as confused as possible for the preservation of the whole uneasy balance."

"I find that the three major administrative problems on a campus are sex for the students, athletics for the alumni and parking for the faculty."

MAY 18

International Museum Day
"Malum vas non frangitur." (Latin) A bad vase doesn't break.

"An antique is something that's been useless so long it's still in pretty good condition."—*Franklin P. Jones, American attorney, born 1906 (birth date not available)*

Bertrand (Arthur William) Russell, *English philosopher and mathematician, born May 18, 1872*
"Our great democracies still tend to think that a stupid man is more likely to be honest than a clever man, and our politicians take advantage of this prejudice by pretending to be even more stupid than nature has made them."

"Organic life has developed gradually from the protozoon to the philosopher and this development, we are assured, is indubitably an advancement. Unfortunately it is the philosopher, not the protozoon, who gives the assurance."

"Even in civilized mankind faint traces of monogamous instinct can be perceived."

"The place of the father in the modern suburban family is a very small one, particularly if he plays golf."

"Even when all the experts agree, they may well be mistaken."

"Mathematics may be defined as the subject in which we never know what we are talking about, nor whether what we are saying is true."

Herbert V(ictor) Prochnow (Sr.), *American speechwriter, editor, humorist, economist, teacher, writer and anthologist, born May 18, 1897*
"The fellow who never makes a mistake takes his orders from one who does."

MAY 19

(Lady) Nancy Astor, *English politician (first woman to sit in British Parliament), born Nancy Witcher Langhorne, May 19, 1879*
"Viscount Waldorf Astor owned Britain's two most influential newspapers, *The Times* and the *Observer*, but his American wife, Nancy, had a wider circulation than both papers put together."—*Emery Kelen about Nancy Astor*

"Nancy was a devout Christian Scientist, but not a good one. She kept confusing herself with God. She didn't know when to step aside and give God a chance."—*Mrs. Gordon Smith about Nancy Astor*

"The penalty of success is to be bored by people who used to snub you."

"In passing, also, I would like to say that the first time Adam had a chance he laid the blame on women."

"We women do talk too much, but even then we don't tell half we know."

Nora Ephron, *American journalist, writer and editor, born May 19, 1941*
"In my sex fantasy, nobody ever loves me for my mind."

MAY 20

Weights and Measures Day
International treaty to establish International Bureau of Weights and Measures signed May 20, 1875.

"The tongue is but three inches long, yet it can kill a man six feet high."—*Japanese saying*

Weights and Measures Day

"Learn this and you'll get along, no matter what your situation: An ounce of keep-your-mouth-shut beats a ton of explanation."—*Anon.*

Generally, the length of a person's foot is equal to the height of his head. (Then how do we get our foot in our mouth so often?)

Honoré de Balzac, *French novelist, born Honoré Balssa, May 20, 1799*
"It takes a nonentity to think of everything."

"I do not regard a broker as a member of the human race."

"A husband should never let his wife visit her mother unattended."

John Stuart Mill, *English philosopher and economist, born May 20, 1806*
"Almost all rich veins of original and striking speculation have been opened by systematic half-thinkers."

Moshe Dayan, *Israeli statesman, born May 20, 1915*
"When you accept our views we shall be in full agreement with you."

Cher, *American singer and actress, born Cherilyn LaPiere, May 20, 1946*
"The trouble with some women is that they get all excited about nothing—and then marry him."

MAY 21

Alexander Pope, *English poet, translator and critic, born May 21, 1688*
"I never knew any man in my life who could not bear another's misfortunes perfectly like a Christian."

"Authors, like coins, grow dear as they grow old;
It is the rust we value, not the gold."

Harold Robbins, *American novelist, born Francis Kane, May 21, 1916*
"Harold could be the best conversationalist in the world—if he ever found anyone he thought worth talking to."—*Herbert Alexander about Harold Robbins*

MAY 22

National Maritime Day
Commemorates departure of SS *Savannah* (from Savannah, GA) on the first successful transatlantic voyage under steam propulsion May 22, 1819

"Old sailors never quit; they just get a little dinghy."—*Anon.*

(Sir) Arthur Conan Doyle, *Scottish physician, novelist and writer, born May 22, 1859*
"A study of family portraits is enough to convert a man to the theory of reincarnation."

Vance (Oakley) Packard, *American writer, born May 22, 1914*
"Rock and roll might be summed up as monotony tinged with hysteria."

Charles Aznavour, *French composer, singer and actor, born May 22, 1924*
"Success is the result of a collective hallucination simulated by the artist."

Robert Byrne, *American writer, born May 22, 1930*
"Getting caught is the mother of invention."

"Learning to dislike children at an early age saves a lot of expense and aggravation later in life."

MAY 23

Ambrose E(verett) Burnside, *American soldier and politician, born May 23, 1824*
"Only Burnside could have managed such a coup, wringing one last spectacular defeat from the jaws of victory."—*Abraham Lincoln about Ambrose E. Burnside*

Douglas Fairbanks, *American actor and producer, born Douglas Eltan Ulman, May 23, 1883*
"The best movie actors are children and animals."

MAY 24

Gardeners' Day
"Gardeners believe in plant parenthood."—*Anon.*

Advertisement by a landscape gardening firm: "Don't kill yourself in your garden. Let us do it for you."

"My garden will never make me famous
I'm still a horticultural ignoramus
I can't tell a stringbean from a soy bean
Or even a girl bean from a boy bean."—*Ogden Nash*

MAY 25

Ralph Waldo Emerson, *American essayist, poet and philosopher, born May 25, 1803*
"I could ... see in Emerson ... that had he lived in those days when the world was made, he might have offered some valuable suggestions."—*Herman Melville about Ralph Waldo Emerson*

"Sometimes a scream is better than a thesis."

"The book written against fame and learning has the author's name on the title page."

"With consistency a great soul has simply nothing to do."

"Among provocatives, the next best thing to good preaching is bad preaching. I have even more thoughts during or enduring it than at other times."

Bennett (Alfred) Cerf, *American publisher, editor, columnist and humorist, born May 25, 1898*
"Incongruous: Where our laws are made."

"Oratory is the art of making a loud noise sound like a deep thought."

MAY 26

(Lady) Mary Wortley Montagu, *English poet, essayist and letter writer, baptized May 26, 1689 (birth date not available)*
"I give myself sometimes admirable advice, but I am incapable of taking it."

John Wayne, *American actor, born Marion Michael Morrison,*
May 26, 1907
> Advice on acting: "Talk low, talk slow, and don't say too much."

> "Women have a right to work—wherever they want to—as long as they have dinner ready when you get home."

> "Nobody likes my acting except the public."

Robert Morley, *English actor, director and playwright, born*
May 26, 1908
> "Anybody who works is a fool. I don't work. I merely inflict myself on the public."

> "The British tourist is always happy abroad so long as the natives are waiters."

> "My future is safe in three-dimensional films."

MAY 27

(Enoch) Arnold Bennett, *English novelist and playwright, born*
May 27, 1867
> "The price of justice is eternal publicity."

> "Good taste is better than bad taste, but bad taste is better than no taste at all."

Hubert H(oratio) Humphrey, *American pharmacist, politician and*
38th US Vice President, born May 27, 1911
> "I don't know what sort of president he'd make. He talks and talks and talks. He'd make a helluva wife."—*Groucho Marx about Hubert H. Humphrey*

> "Behind every successful man stands a surprised mother-in-law."

Vincent Price, *American actor, born May 27, 1911*
> "Nobody would be in this business if he were normal."

> "They'll have to bury me before I retire, and even then my tombstone will read: 'I'll be back!' "

(Arthur) Mervyn Stockwood, *English clergyman and writer, born*
May 27, 1913
> "A psychiatrist is a man who goes to the Folies Bergère to look at the audience."

Herman Wouk, *American novelist, born May 27, 1915*
> "Income tax returns are the most imaginative fiction being written today."

Henry (Alfred) Kissinger, *American political scientist and US Secretary of State, born May 27, 1923*
> "Henry's idea of sex is to slow the car down to thirty miles an hour

when he drops you off at the door."—*Barbara Howar about Henry Kissinger*

"Ninety percent of the politicians give the other ten percent a bad reputation."

"Nobody will ever win the battle of the sexes. There's just too much fraternizing with the enemy."

MAY 28

"Tom" (Thomas Jefferson) Scott, *American composer, singer and musician, born May 28, 1912*

On New Zealand: "Terrible Tragedy in the South Seas. Three million people trapped alive!"

Barry Commoner, *American biologist, ecologist and educator, born May 28, 1917*

"If you can see the light at the end of the tunnel you are looking the wrong way."

MAY 29

G(ilbert) K(eith) Chesterton, *English journalist, essayist, novelist, poet and critic, born May 29, 1874*

"Democracy means government by the uneducated, while aristocracy means government by the badly educated."

"The great and very obvious merit of the English aristocracy is that nobody could possibly take it seriously."

"Angels can fly because they take themselves lightly."

"Journalism largely consists in saying 'Lord Jones is dead' to people who never knew Lord Jones was alive."

"Thieves respect property. They merely wish the property to become their property that they may more perfectly respect it."

"The artistic temperament is a disease that afflicts amateurs."

"What a glorious garden of wonders the lights of Broadway would be to anyone lucky enough to be unable to read."

"Progress is merely a metaphor for walking along a road—very likely the wrong road."

"Every politician is emphatically a promising politician."

"Poets have been mysteriously silent on the subject of cheese."

"A good novel tells us the truth about its hero; but a bad novel tells us the truth about its author."

Bob Hope, *American actor and comedian, born Leslie Townes Hope, May 29, 1903*

"Concorde is great. It gives you three extra hours to find your luggage."

"I love to go to Washington [DC]—if only to be near my money."

"I've always felt England was a great place to work in. It's an island and the audience can't run very far."

"You know you're getting older when the candles cost more than the cake."

"People who throw kisses are hopelessly lazy."

"If you watch a game, that's fun. If you play it, that's recreation. But if you work at it, that's golf."

"My ankles crunch, my knees crunch, my stomach gurgles constantly. I'm not getting older—I'm getting noisier."

"When I look into a girl's eyes I can tell just what she thinks of me. It's pretty depressing."

John F(itzgerald) Kennedy, *American politician, writer and 35th US President, born May 29, 1917*

"When we got into office the thing that surprised me most was to find that things were just as bad as we'd been saying they were."

Paul (Ralph) Ehrlich, *American biologist, educator and writer, born May 29, 1932*

"To err is human but to really foul things up requires a computer."

"I have never believed that science should take time away from chasing women and drinking."

MAY 30

Irving (Grant) Thalberg, *American producer and film executive, born May 30, 1899*

"I don't think this picture could survive a lot of improvement."

"What's all this business about being a writer? It's just putting one word after another."

Cornelia Otis Skinner, *American actress, playwright, essayist and writer, born May 30, 1901*

"Woman's virtue is man's greatest invention."

"One learns in life to keep silent and draws one's own confusions."

MAY 31

"Walt" (Walter) Whitman, *American poet, journalist and essayist, born May 31, 1819*

"I am as bad as the worst, but, thank God, I am as good as the best."

Fred Allen, *American comedian and radio-script writer, born John Florence Sullivan, May 31, 1894*

"The town was so dull that when the tide went out it refused to come back."

"What's on your mind, if you will allow the overstatement?"

"California is a great place—if you happen to be an orange."

"You can take all the sincerity in Hollywood, place it in the navel of a fruit fly and still have room enough for three caraway seeds and a producer's heart."

Advertising agency: "85 percent confusion and 15 percent commission."

"To a newspaperman a human being is an item with skin wrapped around it."

"I have just returned from Boston. It is the only thing to do if you find yourself there."

"A conference is a gathering of important people who singly can do nothing, but together can decide that nothing can be done."

"Television is a medium because well done is rare."

"Imitation is the sincerest form of television."

Television: "A device that permits people who haven't anything to do to watch people who can't do anything."

"I like long walks, especially when they're taken by people who annoy me."

Clint Eastwood, *American actor, producer and director, born May 31, 1930*

"Actually I'm eighteen. I've just lived hard."

John G(eoffrey) Roche, *American publishing executive, born May 31, 1938*

"My ideal business operation is modeled on a pirate ship: if everyone works together, they all share in the booty; if not, they all walk the plank."

June

Dairy Month

Dairy Month
National Rose Month

> "Why is it no one ever sent me yet
> One perfect limousine, do you suppose?
> Ah no, it's always just my luck to get
> One perfect rose."—*Dorothy Parker*

97

"FLOATING" HOLIDAYS THIS MONTH

National Safe Boating Week first week, Sunday thru Saturday
> "A superior sailor is one who uses his superior judgment to keep out of situations requiring the use of his superior skills."—*Anon.*

National Little League Baseball Week Monday thru Sunday, beginning the second Monday

Donut Day first Friday

Father's Day third Sunday
> "A father is a banker provided by nature."—*Anon.*

> "A fool and his father's money—can go places."—*Anon.*

> "When asked why he did not become a father, Thales answered, 'Because I am fond of children.' "—*Diogenes Laertius, Greek biographer*

> "A las días más felices de mi vida, cuando estuve en los brazos de un hombre de otra mujer—mi padre." (Spanish toast) To the happiest days of my life, when I was in the arms of the man of another woman—my father.

> A Michigan State University study in the early 1980's found that given the choice of getting rid of their televisions or their fathers, 35 percent of four- and five-year-olds elected to dispense with Dad.

World Sauntering Day third Friday
> "Walking isn't a lost art—one must, by some means, get to the garage."—*Evan Esar, American writer and anthologist, born 1899 (birth date not available)*

Summer Solstice in Northern Hemisphere (Summer begins) about Jun 22
> "The coldest winter I ever spent was a summer in San Francisco."
> —*Mark Twain*

JUNE 1

Marilyn Monroe, *American actress, born Norma Jean Mortenson, Jun 1, 1926*
> "I am always running into people's unconscious."

> "Television sets should be taken out of bedrooms."

> "The trouble with the censor is that he worries if a girl has cleavage. He should worry if she hasn't any."

> "It's not really me that's late; it's the others who are always in a hurry."

> "What did I put on for sleeping? Chanel No. 5."

> "I have too many fantasies to be a housewife. I guess I am a fantasy."

JUNE 2

Egomaniacs' Day

"La superbia andò a cavallo e tornò a piedi" (Italian saying). Pride rode out on horseback and came back on foot.

"It is almost impossible to find those who admire us entirely lacking in taste."—*Anon.*

"We are not without accomplishment. We have managed to distribute poverty equally."—*Nguyen Co Thach, Vietnamese Foreign Minister (birth date not available)*

Nubar (Sarkis) Gulbenkian, *Iranian oil man and financier, born Jun 2, 1896*

"The best number for a dinner party is two—myself and a damn good head waiter."

JUNE 3

Sydney Smith, *English clergyman, essayist and wit, born Jun 3, 1771*
"Soup and fish explain half the emotions of life."

"Madam, I have been looking for a person who disliked gravy all my life: let us swear eternal friendship."

"Serenely full the Epicure may say—
Fate cannot harm me—I have dined today."

"His enemies might have said before that he talked rather too much; but now he has occasional flashes of silence that make his conversation perfectly delightful."

"I never read a book before reviewing it. It prejudices one so."

Tony Curtis, *American actor, born Bernard Schwartz, Jun 3, 1925*

"He is, in my book, a passionate amoeba."—*David Susskind about Tony Curtis*

JUNE 4

Salesmen's Day

"Old salesmen never quit; they just get out of commission."—*Anon.*

"Ne vendez pas la peau de l'ours avant de l'avoir tué." (French saying). Don't sell the bearskin before you've killed the bear.

"The superior man understands what is right; the inferior man understands what will sell."—*Confucius, Chinese teacher and philosopher*

JUNE 5

World Environment Day
United Nations Conference on the Human Environment opened in
Stockholm, Sweden, Jun 5, 1972.

"There is no economy in going to bed early to save electricity if the
result be twins."—*Chinese proverb*

John Maynard Keynes, *English economist, journalist and financier,*
born Jun 5, 1883
"Regarded as a means, the businessman is tolerable; regarded as
an end he is not so satisfactory."

"Practical men, who believe themselves to be quite exempt from
any intellectual influences, are usually the slaves of some defunct
economist."

"The avoidance of taxes is the only intellectual pursuit that still
carries any reward."

JUNE 6

William Ralph Inge, *English clergyman and writer, born Jun 6, 1860*
"Events in the past may roughly be divided into those which probably never happened and those which do not matter."

"I have never understood why it should be considered derogatory to
the Creator to suppose that he has a sense of humor."

Maria Montez, *Spanish actress, born Maria Antonia Garcia Vidal de*
Santo Silas, Jun 6, 1918
"My legs are so good pipple theenk they must be American."

JUNE 7

(Eugène-Henri-)Paul Gauguin, *French painter, born Jun 7, 1848*
"Life being what it is, one dreams of revenge."

Samuel McChord Crothers, *American clergyman and writer,*
born Jun 7, 1857
"The trouble with facts is that there are so many of them."

JUNE 8

Architects' Day

Frank Lloyd Wright, *American architect and writer, born Jun 8, 1867*

"The doctor can bury his mistakes but an architect can only advise his client to plant vines."

Joan Rivers, *American comedienne, born Joan Sandra Molinsky, Jun 8, 1933*

"I have so little sex appeal that my gynecologist calls me 'sir.' "

JUNE 9

Stay Home Day

John Howard Payne, *American actor, playwright and diplomat (author of "Home, Sweet Home"), born Jun 9, 1791*

"Let others delight 'mid new pleasures to roam,
But give me, oh, give me, the pleasures of home."

Jackie Mason, *American rabbi, comedian, actor and writer, born Yacov Moshe Maza, Jun 9, 1934*

"I have enough money to last me the rest of my life, unless I buy something."

"Eighty percent of married men cheat in America. The rest cheat in Europe."

JUNE 10

Saul Bellow, *American novelist, born Jun 10, 1915*

"The presidency is now a cross between a popularity contest and a high school debate, with an encyclopedia of clichés as the first prize."

Prince Philip, *English royalty (husband of Queen Elizabeth II), born Jun 10, 1921*

"Dentopedology is the science of opening your mouth and putting your foot in it. I've been practising it for years."

JUNE 11

"Vince" (Vincent Thomas) Lombardi, *American football coach, born Jun 11, 1913*

"If you aren't fired with enthusiasm, you will be fired with enthusiasm."

Hazel (Dorothy) Scott, *American jazz pianist and singer, born Jun 11, 1920*

"There's a time when you have to explain to your children why they're born, and it's a marvelous thing if you know the reason by then."

JUNE 12

Gossip Day

"When you hear that someone has gossiped of you, kindly reply that he did not know the rest of your faults or he would not have mentioned only these."—*Anon.*

"You can never tell about a woman, and if you can, you shouldn't."—*Anon.*

"Knowledge is power—especially if you know about the right people."—*Anon.*

"Another good thing about gossip is that it is within everybody's reach, And it is much more interesting than any other form of speech."
—*Ogden Nash*

Gossip Day

JUNE 13

William Butler Yeats, *Irish poet, playwright, essayist and politician, born Jun 13, 1865*
"The worst thing about some men is that when they are not drunk they are sober."

Allen P(arker) Stults, *American banker, born Jun 13, 1913*
"Our problems are mostly behind us—what we have to do now is fight the solutions."

JUNE 14

Flag Day in United States

National Flag Week in United States the week, Sunday thru Saturday, that includes June 14

Fashion Designer's Day
"Aunque el mono se vista de seda, mono se queda." (Spanish saying). A monkey dressed in silk is still a monkey.

"Wearing shorts usually reveals nothing about a man so much as his indifference to public opinion."—*Franklin P. Jones, American attorney, born 1906 (birth date not available)*

"Women's styles may change, but their designs remain the same." —*Anon.*

The Rules of Entry for the Miss Nude USA Competition included the stipulation that contestants must show "taste in clothing."

JUNE 15

Ignorance Day
The political platform of the Know-Nothing Party was published Jun 15, 1855. (Republicans and Democrats are still using it.)

"Common sense in an uncommon degree is what the world calls wisdom."—*Anon.*

"Half the misery in the world is caused by ignorance. The other half is caused by knowledge."—*Bonar Thompson, English actor, broadcaster, editor and writer, born 1888 (birth date not available)*

Herman ("Jackrabbit") Smith-Johannsen, *Canadian skier, born Jun 15, 1875*
At age 103: "The secret to a long life is to stay busy, get plenty of exercise and don't drink too much. Then again, don't drink too little."

JUNE 16

Lovers' Day

"Love: softening of the heartery."—*Anon.*

"The first sigh of love is the last of wisdom."—*Antoine Bret, French writer and poet, born 1717 (birth date not available)*

"Amour fait rage, mais argent fait mariage" (French saying). Love makes rage, but money makes marriages.

"When you are in love with someone you want to be near him all the time, except when you are out buying things and charging them to him."—*Miss Piggy, Muppet actress*

"Loin des yeux, loin du coeur" (French saying). Far from eyes, far from heart.

"Love and eggs are best when they are fresh."—*Russian proverb*

"Celibacy is never having to say you're boring."—*Gabrielle Brown, American writer (birth date not available)*

"Sex is a misdemeanor: The less you have, de meaner you get."
  —*Charles Pierce (biographical information not available)*

  "Any kiddie in school can love like a fool
  But hating, my boy, is an art."—*Ogden Nash*

JUNE 17

Igor (Fyodorovich) Stravinsky, *Russian-American composer, born Jun 17, 1882*

"His music used to be original. Now it is aboriginal."
  —*Ernest Newman about Igor Stravinsky*

"Too many pieces of music finish too long after the end."

"My music is best understood by children and animals."

Dean Martin, *American singer and actor, born Dino Crocetti, Jun 17, 1917*

"If you drink, don't drive. Don't even putt."

"The only reason I drink is because when I am sober I think I am Eddie Fisher."

Elroy "Crazylegs" (Leon) Hirsch, *American football player and sports administrator, born Jun 17, 1923*

"Hollywood made a movie of my life. The film had me proposing to my wife on the football field. I would never misuse a football field that way."

JUNE 18

Hooray for Hollywood Day

"Keep it out of focus. I want to win the foreign-picture award."
—*Billy Wilder*

"No one has his ups and downs like the person in the end seat at the theatre."—*Anon.*

"The difference between Los Angeles and yogurt is that yogurt has an active, living culture."—*Anon.*

"Hollywood is a locality where people without reputation try to live up to it."—*Anon.*

"Hollywood is a carnival where there are no concessions."—*Anon.*

"Hollywood: the land of yes-men and acqui-yes girls."—*Anon.*

"Why should people go out and pay money to see bad films when they can stay home and see bad television for nothing?"—*Samuel Goldwyn*

Hooray for Hollywood Day

JUNE 19

Thomas Fuller, *English scholar, preacher, historian and biographer,*
born Jun 19, 1608
"He that knows little often repeats it."

"Many have been the wise speeches of fools, though not so many as
the foolish speeches of wise men."

Blaise Pascal, *French philosopher, mathematician, physicist and*
writer, born Jun 19, 1623
"Had Cleopatra's nose been shorter, the whole history of the world
would have been different."

"I have made this letter longer than usual, because I lack the time
to make it short."

"Continuous eloquence is tedious."

"It is not certain that everything is uncertain."

Elbert (Green) Hubbard, *American journalist, editor, publisher and*
writer, born Jun 19, 1856
"A pessimist is a man who has been compelled to live with an
optimist."

"When a fellow says, 'It ain't the money, but the principle of the
thing,' it's the money."

"The world is moving so fast these days that the man who says it
can't be done is generally interrupted by someone doing it."

Elisabeth Marbury, *American producer, agent and writer, born*
Jun 19, 1856
"The richer your friends, the more they will cost you."

Duchess of Windsor ("Wally" Simpson), *American divorcée for*
whom Edward VIII abdicated, born Bessie Wallis Warfield,
Jun 19, 1896
"I would like to be the head of an advertising agency."

Guy (Albert) Lombardo, *Canadian band leader, born Jun 19, 1902*
"Many a man wishes he were strong enough to tear a telephone
book in half—especially if he has a teenage daughter."

JUNE 20

Lillian Hellman, *American playwright, born Jun 20, 1905*
"It is best in the theatre to act with confidence no matter how little
right you have to it."

"History people make themselves; cooking they have to learn."

"I cannot and will not cut my conscience to fit this year's fashions."

Errol (Leslie Thomson) Flynn, *American actor, born Jun 20, 1909*
"The rest of my life will be devoted to women and litigation."

"My problem lies in reconciling my gross habits with my net income."

Anne Murray, *Canadian singer, born Jun 20, 1945*
"My image has been the wholesome girl-next-door, apple-cheek-Annie thing.... Behind this facade, this body is a mass of hickeys."

JUNE 21

Jean-Paul Sartre, *French novelist, playwright and philosopher, born Jun 21, 1905*
"Everything has been figured out except how to live."

Jane Russell, *American actress, born Jun 21, 1921*
"There are two reasons why men go to see Jane Russell. Those are enough."—*Howard Hughes about Jane Russell*

Françoise Sagan, *French novelist, born Françoise Quoirez, Jun 21, 1935*
"I like men to behave like men—strong and childish."

JUNE 22

Anne Morrow Lindbergh, *American aviator, poet and writer, born Jun 22, 1906*
"By and large, mothers and housewives are the only workers who do not have regular time off. They are the great vacationless class."

Billy Wilder, *American producer, director and writer, born Samuel Wilder, Jun 22, 1906*
"Beneath Billy Wilder's aggressive gruff exterior is pure Brillo."
—*Harry Kurnitz about Billy Wilder*

"I'd worship the ground you walked on if only you lived in a better neighborhood."

On the advent of television: "I'm delighted with it, because it used to be that films were the lowest form of art. Now we've got something to look down on."

Freddie Prinze, *American actor and comedian, born Jun 22, 1954*
"My folks met on the subway trying to pick each other's pockets."

JUNE 23

Irvin S(hrewsbury) Cobb, *American journalist, humorist, editor and playwright, born Jun 23, 1876*
"If writers were good businessmen, they'd have too much sense to be writers."

Alfred (Charles) Kinsey, *American zoologist and sexologist, born Jun 23, 1894*

"I hardly see him at night since he took up sex."—*Mrs. Kinsey about her husband, Alfred Kinsey*

Duke of Windsor (Edward Albert Christian George Andrew Patrick David), *English royalty (was King Edward VIII before abdicating), born Jun 23, 1894*

"The thing that impresses me most about America is the way parents obey their children."

JUNE 24

Ambrose (Gwinnett) Bierce, *American journalist, short-story writer and satirist, born Jun 24, 1842*

"Don't steal; thou'lt never thus compete
Successfully in business. Cheat."

"Speak when you are angry and you will make the best speech you will ever regret."

"Appeal: In law, to put the dice into the box for another throw."

"Here's to woman! Would that we could fall into her arms without falling into her hands."

"The gambling known as business looks with severe disfavor upon the business known as gambling."

"Cabbage: A ... vegetable about as large and wise as a man's head."

"Woman: An animal ... having a rudimentary susceptibility to domestication.... The species is the most widely distributed of all beasts of prey.... The woman is omnivorous and can be taught not to talk."

Logic: "The art of thinking and reasoning in strict accordance with the limitations and incapacities of the human understanding."

Painting: "The art of protecting flat surfaces from the weather and exposing them to the critic."

"Acquaintance: a degree of friendship called slight when the object is poor or obscure, and intimate when he is rich or famous."

"To consult is to seek another's advice on a course already decided upon."

"The covers of this book are too far apart."

"Love—A temporary insanity curable by marriage."

"Abstainer: a weak person who yields to the temptation of denying himself a pleasure."

"Admiration: our polite recognition of another man's resemblance to ourselves."

"Egotist: A person ... more interested in himself than in me."

Noise: "The chief product and authenticating sign of civilization."

"Liberty: One of Imagination's most precious possessions."

Phil Harris, *American actor and band leader, born Jun 24, 1906*
"I can't die until the government finds a safe place to bury my liver."

John (Anthony) Ciardi, *American poet, translator and critic, born Jun 24, 1916*
"Modern art is what happens when painters stop looking at girls and persuade themselves that they have a better idea."

Claude Chabrol, *French director, born Jun 24, 1930*
"Foolishness is infinitely more fascinating than intelligence.... Intelligence has limits while foolishness has none."

JUNE 25

(Sir) Ernest (John Pickstone) Benn, *English publisher, born Jun 25, 1875*
"Politics is the art of looking for trouble, finding it whether it exists or not, diagnosing it incorrectly, and applying the wrong remedy."

George Orwell, *English journalist, novelist, essayist and critic, born Eric Arthur Blair, Jun 25, 1903*
"Advertising is the rattling of a stick inside a swill bucket."

"Autobiography is only to be trusted when it reveals something disgraceful."

"No doubt alcohol, tobacco, and so forth, are things that a saint must avoid, but sainthood is also a thing that human beings must avoid."

"All animals are equal, but some animals are more equal than others."

Sidney Lumet, *American director, born Jun 25, 1924*
"Directors are no different than anybody else; their capacity for self-deception is enormous."

JUNE 26

Pearl S(ydenstricker) Buck, *American novelist, born Jun 26, 1892*
"It is indeed exasperating to have a memory that begins too young and continues too long."

Peter Lorre, *American actor, born László Loewenstein, Jun 26, 1904*
"All you need to imitate me is a pair of soft-boiled eggs and a bedroom voice."

"Babe" Zaharias, *American athlete, born Mildred Ella Didrikson, Jun 26, 1914*

> "When I want to really blast one, I just loosen my girdle and let 'er fly."

JUNE 27

Speakers' Day

> "No speech can be entirely bad if it is short."—*Anon.*

> "Speech is conveniently located midway between thought and action, where it often substitutes for both."—*John Andrew Holmes, American lawyer, born 1812 (birth date not available)*

> "Recipe for a good after-dinner speech: forget the other ingredients, just use plenty of shortening."—*Anon.*

> "Speeches are like steer horns—a point here, a point there and a lot of bull in between."—*Liberty*

JUNE 28

Jean Jacques Rousseau, *French philosopher and writer, born Jun 28, 1712*

> "To write a good love-letter, you ought to begin without knowing what you mean to say, and to finish without knowing what you have written."

Mel Brooks, *American comedy writer, actor, producer and director, born Melvyn Kaminsky, Jun 28, 1926*

> "Bad taste is simply saying the truth before it should be said."

> "Suppose I became the Jean Renoir of America. What the hell would be left for the other guys to do?"

> "I stare at life through fields of mayonnaise."

Gilda Radner, *American comedienne and actress, born Jun 28, 1946*

> "I love being a woman. You can cry. You get to wear pants now.... It must be a great thing, or so many men wouldn't be wanting to do it...."

> "I base my fashion taste on what doesn't itch."

JUNE 29

Antoine(-Marie-Roger) de Saint-Exupéry, *French aviator and writer, born Jun 29, 1900*

> "Grown-ups never understand anything for themselves, and it is tiresome for children to be always and forever explaining things to them."

Joan (Josephine) Davis, *American actress and comedienne, born Jun 29, 1907*

"In the race for love, I was scratched."

JUNE 30

Budgeting Day

"Living on a budget is the same as living beyond your means, except that you have a record of it."—*Anon.*

"Why is there always so much month left at the end of the money?"—*Anon.*

"It's easy to meet expenses—everywhere we go, there they are." —*Anon.*

"Want to estimate the cost of living? Take your income and add twenty percent."—*Anon.*

"Budget: A family's attempt to live below its yearnings."—*Anon.*

"Just about the time you think you can make both ends meet, somebody moves the ends."—*Pansy Penner (biographical information not available)*

"The husband has to make money first and his wife has to make it last."—*Anon.*

"Every family has a choice of keeping up with the neighbors or with the creditors."—*Anon.*

"Money talks all right. Usually it says, 'Goodbye.'"—*Anon.*

July

National Picnic Month

Hitchhiking Month
National Hot Dog Month
National Ice Cream Month
National Recreation and Park Month
National Picnic Month
 The animal with the largest brain in proportion to its body is the

ant, and an ant can lift fifty times its weight. (If they're so smart, why don't they get somebody else to do the work?)

National Anti-Boredom Month
The habit of covering one's mouth when yawning originated from a fear that the soul might leave the body. Recent studies show that yawning may actually *increase* alertness. And yes, yawning is, unexplainably, contagious. (So, try it in your office or home and see how alert everybody becomes.)

"FLOATING" HOLIDAYS THIS MONTH

Man Watchers' Compliment Week first week, Sunday thru Saturday Say something nice to a man.

JULY 1

Canada Day in Canada (observed the following day when July 1 is a Sunday)
"Quebec is one of the ten provinces against which Canada is defending itself."—*Carl Dubuc (biographical information not available)*

Georg Christoph Lichtenberg, *German physicist and satirist, born Jul 1, 1742*
"When a book and a head collide and there is a hollow sound, is it always from the book?"

"There can hardly be a stranger commodity in the world than books. Printed by people who don't understand them; sold by people who don't understand them; bound, criticized and read by people who don't understand them; and now even written by people who don't understand them."

"For a long time now I have thought that philosophy will one day devour itself. Metaphysics has partly done so already."

"Love is blind, but marriage restores its sight."

Olivia (Mary) de Havilland, *American actress, born Jul 1, 1916*
"One must take what comes, with laughter."

JULY 2

Debtors' Day
"The difficult thing is to get out of debt faster than the speed of worry."—*Anon.*

"God forbid that I should be out of debt, as if, indeed, I could not be trusted."—*François Rabelais, French monk, physician and novelist, born c.1483 (birth date not available)*

"Most of us would be willing to pay as we go, if we could just finish paying for where we've been."—*Anon.*

Robert W(illiam) Sarnoff, *American broadcasting executive, born Jul 2, 1918*

"Finance is the art of passing currency from hand to hand until it finally disappears."

JULY 3

Disobedience Day

Dog Days July 3-August 15

In ancient times, a brown dog was sacrificed at the beginning of Dog Days to appease Sirius, the Dog Star, believed to be the cause of the hot, sultry weather. Dog days bright and clear indicate a bounteous year.

Franz Kafka, *German novelist and short-story writer, born Jul 3, 1883*

"Don't despair, not even over the fact that you don't despair."

John Mason Brown, *American editor, critic and writer, born Jul 3, 1900*

"How prophetic L'Enfant was when he laid out Washington [DC] as a city that goes around in circles!"

George Sanders, *American actor, born Jul 3, 1906*

"An actor is not quite a human being—but then who is?"

"I am content with mediocrity."

Tom Stoppard, *English journalist and playwright, born Tom Straussler, Jul 3, 1937*

"My husband only writes about a certain sort of woman. She looks like Marilyn Monroe and has an IQ of 200."—*Miriam Stoppard about Tom Stoppard*

"A foreign correspondent is someone who ... flies around from hotel to hotel and thinks the most interesting thing about any story is the fact that he has arrived to cover it."

"It is better to be quotable than to be honest."

"I think age is a very high price to pay for maturity."

JULY 4

Independence Day in United States

"Democracy is like a raft: It won't sink, but you will always have your feet wet."—*Anon.*

Disobedience Day

Nathaniel Hawthorne, *American novelist, born Jul 4, 1804*
He always washed his hands before sitting down to read a letter from his wife.

(John) Calvin ("Silent Cal") Coolidge, *American lawyer and 30th US President, born Jul 4, 1872*
"He had one really notable talent. He slept more than any other president."—*H.L. Mencken about Calvin Coolidge*

"Calvin Coolidge didn't say much, and when he did he didn't say much."—*Will Rogers about Calvin Coolidge*

"If you don't say anything you won't be called on to repeat it."

"When a great many people are unable to find work, unemployment results."

"I have noticed that nothing I never said ever did me any harm."

George M(ichael) Cohan, *American actor, songwriter, playwright and producer, born Jul 4, 1878*
"Many a bum show has been saved by the flag."

"Rube" (Reuben Lucius) Goldberg, *American cartoonist, engineer, sportswriter and sculptor, born Jul 4, 1883*
> "A touch of art may nourish the soul, but a good laugh always aids the digestion."

Louis B. Mayer, *American producer and film executive, born Jul 4, 1885*
> "He's done more for movies than dark balconies."—*Anon. about Louis B. Mayer*

> About the crowd at Mayer's funeral: "It only proves what they always say—give the public something they want to see, and they'll come out for it."—*Red Skelton about Louis B. Mayer*

Louis (Daniel) ("Satchmo") Armstrong, *American musician, born Jul 4, 1900*
> Asked to define jazz: "Man, if you gotta ask you'll never know."

> He signed his letters, "Red beans and ricely yours."

Ann Landers, *American advice columnist, born Esther Pauline Friedman, Jul 4, 1918*
> "Television has proved that people will look at anything rather than each other."

Abigail Van Buren, *American advice columnist, born Pauline Esther Friedman, Jul 4, 1918*
> "In Biblical times, a man could have as many wives as he could afford. Just like today."

> "Accept every blind date you can get, even with a girl who wears jeans. Maybe you can talk her out of them."

> "It is true that I was born in Iowa, but I can't speak for my twin sister."

(Marvin) Neil Simon, *American playwright, born Jul 4, 1927*
> "I've already had medical attention—a dog licked me when I was on the ground."

Geraldo Rivera, *American lawyer, broadcast journalist and writer, born Jul 4, 1943*
> "If Geraldo Rivera is the first journalist in space, NASA can test the effect of weightlessness on weightlessness."—*Anon. about Geraldo Rivera*

JULY 5

Jean Cocteau, *French poet, novelist, librettist, painter, actor, director and filmmaker, born Jul 5, 1889*
> "The cinema has thawed out people's brains."

> "We must believe in luck. For how else can we explain the success of those we don't like?"

> "Tact consists in knowing how far to go too far."

"Since these mysteries exceed my grasp, I shall pretend to have organized them."

JULY 6

Nancy (Davis) Reagan, *American actress, wife of 40th US President, born Anne Frances Robbins, Jul 6, 1923*
"Nancy Reagan has agreed to be the first artificial heart donor."
  —*Andrea C. Michaels about Nancy Reagan*

"I still think Nancy does most of Reagan's talking; you'll notice that she never drinks water when Ronnie speaks."—*Robin Williams about Nancy Reagan*

"A woman is like a tea bag; you don't know her strength until she is in hot water."

"I believe that people would be alive today if there were a death penalty."

JULY 7

Manufacturers' Day
"We are all manufacturers: making goods, making trouble, making excuses."—*Anon.*

"Behold the guarantee—the bold print giveth, and the fine print taketh away."—*Anon.*

Robert (Anson) Heinlein, *American science-fiction writer, born Jul 7, 1907*
"An elephant—a mouse built to government specifications."

JULY 8

Plan Your Vacation Day
First US passport issued Jul 8, 1796
"If you look like your passport photo, you're too sick to travel."—*Anon.*

"It's when you're safe at home that you wish you were having an adventure. When you're having an adventure you wish you were safe at home."—*Anon.*

"Adventure is the result of poor planning."—*Col. Blatchford Snell (biographical information not available)*

"Travel tip: Keep two bags very full—one of patience and the other of money."—*Anon.*

Plan Your Vacation Day

JULY 9

Ernest Dimnet, *French priest and writer, born Jul 9, 1866*
  "Artists hate the enlightened amateur unless he buys."

Don Herold, *American writer and cartoonist, born Jul 9, 1889*
  "I say, let's banish bridge; let's find some pleasanter way of being miserable together."

Covert Bailey, *American writer, lecturer and critic, born Jul 9, 1932*
  "No diet will remove all the fat from your body because the brain is entirely fat. Without a brain you might look good, but all you could do is run for public office."

JULY 10

Finley Peter Dunne, *American journalist and humorist, born Jul 10, 1867*
  "Many a man that couldn't direct ye to th' drug store on th' corner

when he was thirty will get a respectful hearin' when age has further impaired his mind."

"Miracles are laughed at by a nation that reads thirty million newspapers a day and supports Wall Street."

Marcel Proust, *French novelist, born Jul 10, 1871*
"Impelled by a state of mind which is destined not to last, we make our irrevocable decisions."

"Everybody calls 'clear' those ideas which have the same degree of confusion as his own."

"There is nothing like desire for preventing the things we say from having any resemblance to the things in our minds."

"A work in which there are theories is like an object which still has its price-tag on it."

"An absence, the declining of an invitation to dinner, an unintentional, unconscious harshness are of more service than all the cosmetics and fine clothes in the world."

E(dmund) C(lerihew) Bentley, *English journalist, poet and novelist, born Jul 10, 1875*
> "The art of Biography
> Is different from Geography
> Geography is about maps
> Biography is about chaps."

(Sir) Kenneth (MacKenzie) Clark, *English teacher, art historian and writer, born Jul 10, 1903*
"Opera, next to Gothic architecture, is one of the strangest inventions of modern man. It could not have been foreseen by any logical process."

Jean Kerr, *American playwright, born Jean Collins, Jul 10, 1923*
"Hope is the feeling you have that the feeling you have isn't permanent."

"If you can keep your head when all about you are losing theirs, it's just possible you haven't grasped the situation."

"Women speak because they wish to speak, whereas a man speaks only when driven to speech by something outside himself—like, for instance, he can't find any clean socks."

JULY 11

Censors' Day
   Thomas Bowdler, *English doctor and self-appointed literary censor, born Jul 11, 1754*
   He rewrote the works of Shakespeare and other authors, removing

what he considered offensive words. Hence the word "bowdlerize."

"If you don't expose your morals
You'll avoid the censor's quarrels."—*Eileen Mason*

John Wanamaker, *American merchant, philanthropist and US Post-master General, born Jul 11, 1838*
"Half the money I spend on advertising is wasted, and the trouble is I don't know which half."

E(lwyn) B(rooks) White, *American essayist, novelist and humorist, born Jul 11, 1899*
"Be obscure clearly."

Blake Clark, *American editor, writer and business executive, born Jul 11, 1908*
"Being in the army is like being in the Boy Scouts, except that the Boy Scouts have adult supervision."

Yul Brynner, *American actor, born Taidje Khan, Jul 11, 1920*
"Girls have an unfair advantage over men: If they can't get what they want by being smart, they can get it by being dumb."

Tab Hunter, *American actor, born Arthur Gelien, Jul 11, 1931*
"I'm typical of where publicity is a zillion years ahead of career."

"Jerry" (Jerome Lee) Herman, *American restaurateur, born Jul 11, 1933*
"My wife has every degree there is except one—a J.O.B."

JULY 12

Henry (David) Thoreau, *American essayist, poet and philosopher, born Jul 12, 1817*
"Distrust any enterprise that requires new clothes."

"Men have become the tools of their tools."

On Apr 30, 1844, on a fishing trip near Concord, he accidentally set fire to the woods, burning 300 acres.

R(ichard) Buckminster Fuller, *American engineer, architect, poet and philosopher, born Jul 12, 1895*
"Dare to be naive."

Milton Berle, *American comedian and actor, born Milton Berlinger, Jul 12, 1908*
"A committee is a group that keeps the minutes and loses hours."

JULY 13

Hospitality Day
"If the soup had been as warm as the wine, and the wine as old as

the fish, and the fish as young as the maid, and the maid as willing as the hostess, it would have been a very good meal."—*Anon.*

"Some cause happiness wherever they go; others whenever they go."—*Anon.*

"The hostess was playing the piano when one of the guests said, 'What do you think of her execution?' and another replied, 'I'm in favor of it.' "—*Anon.*

The term "cold shoulder" came from medieval times when guests who overstayed their welcome into the dinner hour were served a platter of cooked, but cold, beef shoulder, to discourage them from doing that again.

JULY 14

Bastille Day
Bastille overtaken (at beginning of French Revolution), Jul 14, 1789.

"France is a place where the money falls apart in your hands but you can't tear the toilet paper."—*Billy Wilder*

James (Abbott McNeill) Whistler, *American painter, etcher and lithographer, born Jul 14, 1834*
"If other people are going to talk, conversation becomes impossible."

"Happy" (Albert Benjamin) Chandler, *American lawyer, politician and US Baseball Commissioner, born Jul 14, 1898*
"I promised [my wife] that if we ever fussed, I would go outside. Fifty-seven years in the open air does wonders for a man's health."

Gerald (Rudolph) Ford (Jr.), *American politician and 38th US President, born Leslie Lynch King, Jr., Jul 14, 1913*
"He played too much football with his helmet off."—*Lyndon Baines Johnson about Gerald Ford*

"I happen to think that the three-martini lunch is the epitome of American efficiency. Where else can you get an earful, a bellyful and a snootful at the same time?"

JULY 15

St. Swithin's Day
Old English belief has it that rain on this day will mean rain for the next forty days, but if it's fair, there will be no rain for forty days.

Clerics' Day
"A priest is a man who is called Father by everyone except his own children, who are obliged to call him Uncle."—*Italian saying*

"We've just started a church. It's non-denominational—we accept twenties, fifties, hundreds—whatever you have."—*Eileen Mason*

Bicycling's increasing popularity was reducing church attendance so much that in 1896 a Baltimore preacher denounced bicycles as "diabolical devices of the demon of darkness."

Coffee was baptized by the Pope in the 17th century to dispel the notion that it was "an invention of the devil." (Wine, however, was always "de vine.")

JULY 16

(Sir) Joshua Reynolds, *English painter, born Jul 16, 1723*
"He who resolves never to ransack any mind but his own will be ... obliged to imitate himself."

Kathleen Norris, *American novelist, born Kathleen Thompson, Jul 16, 1880*
"In spite of the cost of living, it's still popular."

Ginger Rogers, *American dancer and actress, born Virginia Katherine McMath, Jul 16, 1911*
"I live for today, that's why people think I'm strange. I don't even have a psychiatrist."

Leonard Shatzkin, *American teacher, publishing executive and writer, born Jul 16, 1919*
"The wag who said that the camel was the product of a committee was speaking of a very exceptional committee indeed if it was able to produce anything with the breath of life."

On editors: "There are no rubdowns in the editorial locker room and certainly no pep talks. And the players may find themselves tripped by their own coach on their way to the field."

JULY 17

Geographer's Day
On Jul 17, 1938 Douglas Groce Corrigan flew from New York, headed for Los Angeles, and ended up in Ireland the next day, earning the nickname "Wrong Way" Corrigan.

"If you don't know where you're going, you're sure to get there."
—*Eileen Mason*

Christina (Ellen) Stead, *Australian novelist and short-story writer, born Jul 17, 1902*
"If all the rich people in the world divided up their money among themselves there wouldn't be enough to go round."

"If my jeans could talk they'd plead for mercy."

"Art" (Arthur Gordon) Linkletter, *American radio / television host and producer, born Jul 17, 1912*

"The four stages of man are infancy, childhood, adolescence and obsolescence."

Phyllis Diller, *American comedienne, born Phyllis Driver, Jul 17, 1917*

"Never go to bed mad. Stay up and fight."

"Burt Reynolds once asked me out. I was in his room."

"A terrible thing happened again last night—nothing."

"We spend the first twelve months of our children's lives teaching them to walk and talk and the next twelve telling them to sit down and shut up."

"I'll tell you what I don't like about Christmas office parties—looking for a new job afterward."

"My husband wanted a room of his own: He wanted it in Pittsburgh."

"This man I was going with asked me for my finger measurements. I thought he was going to buy me a ring for Christmas, but he gave me a bowling ball."

"It's an ill wind that blows when you leave the hairdresser."

"When I prepare to go to sleep, everything comes off or out."

"If my jeans could talk they'd plead for mercy."

"When I go to the beauty parlor, I always use the emergency entrance. Sometimes I just go for an estimate."

Erwin Knoll, *American journalist, editor, writer and critic, born Jul 17, 1931*
"Everything you read in the newspapers is absolutely true except for the rare story of which you happen to have first-hand knowledge."

JULY 18

William Makepeace Thackeray, *English novelist, born Jul 18, 1811*
"If a man's character is to be abused, say what you will, there's nobody like a relation to do the business."

Philip Snowden, *English politician and writer, born Jul 18, 1864*
"It would be desirable if every government, when it comes to power, should have its old speeches burnt."

Nathalie Sarraute, *French novelist, born Jul 18, 1902*
"Television has lifted the manufacture of banality out of the sphere of handicraft and placed it in that of a major industry."

S(amuel) I(chiyé) Hayakawa, *American politician and educator, born Jul 18, 1906*
"I'm going to speak my mind because I have nothing to lose."

"Red" (Richard Bernard) Skelton, *American comedian and actor, born Jul 18, 1913*
"Congress: Bingo with billions."

JULY 19

A(rchibald) J(oseph) Cronin, *Scottish physician, novelist and playwright, born Jul 19, 1896*
"... Amiability and good temper do not come easily when one is hungry...."

"Sam" (Samuel Robinson) Ogden, *American columnist, politician and writer, born Jul 19, 1896*
"The sooner you fall behind, the more time you have to catch up."

Herbert Marcuse, *American political philosopher, teacher and writer, born Jul 19, 1898*
"Not every problem one has with his girlfriend is necessarily due to the capitalist mode of production."

JULY 20

Space Week the week, Sunday thru Saturday, including Jul 20
American astronaut Commander Neil Armstrong became the first
man to walk on the moon on Jul 20, 1969.

"If they could put one man on the moon, why can't they put them
all?"—*Anon.*

Theda Bara, *American actress, born Theodosia Goodman, Jul 20, 1890*
"The reason good women like me and flock to my pictures is that
there is a little bit of vampire instinct in every woman."

(Sir) Edmund (Percival) Hillary, *New Zealand mountaineer, bee-
keeper and explorer, born Jul 20, 1919*
"The problems and dissensions of multi-national expeditions pale
into insignificance compared to those that can be brought about by
a single woman."

"We climbed [Mt. Everest] because nobody climbed it before."

Natalie Wood, *American actress, born Natasha Gurdin, Jul 20, 1938*
"The only time a woman really succeeds in changing a man is when
he's a baby."

JULY 21

Ernest (Miller) Hemingway, *American novelist, born Jul 21, 1899*
"Real seriousness in regard to writing is one of two absolute neces-
sities. The other, unfortunately, is talent."

"What is moral is what you feel good after."

"He was awake a long time before he remembered that his heart
was broken."

(Herbert) Marshall McLuhan, *Canadian educator and writer, born
Jul 21, 1911*
"Most people are alive in an earlier time...."

"Canada is the only country in the world that knows how to live
without an identity."

JULY 22

Spooner's Day
  William Archibald Spooner, *English clergyman, born Jul 22, 1844*

He was famous for his slips of the tongue, for example (during
World War I): "When the boys come back from France, we'll have
the hags flung out!" Hence the word "spoonerism."

Take Pains with Punctuation Day
>Mariner I, the Venus-bound rocket, suddenly surged off its planned course and had to be exploded Jul 22, 1962, costing United States taxpayers $18.5 million. The reason: A hyphen had been left out of the flight computer program.

JULY 23

Simeon Strunsky, *American journalist, editor, novelist and essayist, born Jul 23, 1879*
>"The beneficent effects of the regular quarter-hour's exercise before breakfast is more than offset by the mental wear-and-tear in getting out of bed fifteen minutes earlier than one otherwise would."

Raymond (Thornton) Chandler, *American novelist and short-story writer, born Jul 23, 1888*
>"Los Angeles is a city with the personality of a paper cup."

>Chess: "As elaborate a waste of human intelligence as you can find outside an advertising agency."

>"If my books had been any worse, I should not have been invited to Hollywood, and if they had been any better, I should not have come."

>"I do a lot of research, especially in the apartments of tall blondes."

JULY 24

Alexandre Dumas (Sr.), *French novelist and playwright, born Jul 24, 1802*
>"Business? It's quite simple. It's other people's money."

>On Jan 5, 1825, he fought his first duel, during which his trousers fell down.

(Lord) Edward John Moreton Drax Plunkett Dunsany, *Irish playwright, short-story writer and poet, born Jul 24, 1878*
>"Humanity, let us say, is like people packed in an automobile which is travelling downhill without lights at a terrific speed and driven by a small four-year-old child. The signposts along the way are all marked 'Progress.'"

JULY 25

(Lord) Arthur James Balfour, *English statesman and Prime Minister, born Jul 25, 1848*
 "London is a splendid place to live in for those who can get out of it."

Eric Hoffer, *American longshoreman, writer and philosopher, born Jul 25, 1902*
 "When people are free to do as they please, they usually imitate each other."

Elias Canetti, *Bulgarian novelist and playwright, born Jul 25, 1905*
 "He would like to start from scratch. Where is scratch?"

JULY 26

George Bernard Shaw, *Irish playwright and literary critic, born Jul 26, 1856*
 "He certainly didn't approve of romance in the ordinary way. He had mad love affairs with women, but always only in letters written for posterity."—*Rex Harrison about George Bernard Shaw*

 "Shaw's works make me admire the magnificent tolerance and broadmindedness of the English."—*James Joyce about George Bernard Shaw*

 "He writes his plays for the ages—the ages between five and twelve."—*George Jean Nathan about George Bernard Shaw*

 "Alcohol is a very necessary article.... It enables Parliament to do things at eleven at night that no sane person would do at eleven in the morning."

 "An Irishman's heart is nothing but his imagination."

 "There is no love sincerer than the love of food."

 "A drama critic is a man who leaves no turn unstoned."

 "Martyrdom is the only way in which a man can become famous without ability."

 "Democracy substitutes election by the incompetent many for appointment by the corrupt few."

 "There are two tragedies in life. One is not to get your heart's desire. The other is to get it."

 "Love consists in overestimating the difference between one woman and another."

 "He knows nothing; he thinks he knows everything—that clearly points to a political career."

 "The faults of the burglar are the qualities of the financier."

"Marriage is popular because it combines the minimum of temptation with the maximum of opportunity."

"The British churchgoer prefers a severe preacher because he thinks a few home truths will do his neighbours no harm."

"The English are not a very spiritual people, so they invented cricket to give them some idea of eternity."

"It took me twenty years of studied self-restraint, aided by the natural decay of my faculties, to make myself dull enough to be accepted as a serious person by the British public."

"I am a millionaire. That is my religion."

"I am a sort of a collector of religions, and the curious thing is I find I can believe in them all."

"If all economists were laid end to end, they would not reach a conclusion."

"Lack of money is the root of all evil."

"I often quote myself; it adds spice to my conversation."

"I'm an atheist, and I thank God for it."

"You must not suppose, because I am a man of letters, that I never tried to earn an honest living."

Carl (Gustav) Jung, *Swiss psychologist and psychiatrist, born Jul 26, 1875*
"Show me a sane man and I will cure him for you."

"The pendulum of the mind oscillates between sense and nonsense, not between right and wrong."

André Maurois, *French biographer, novelist, essayist and critic, born Émile Salomon Wilhelm Herzog, Jul 26, 1885*
"In literature as in love, we are astonished at what is chosen by others."

Aldous (Leonard) Huxley, *English novelist and critic, born Jul 26, 1894*
"Technological progress has merely provided us with more efficient means for going backwards."

"Only a person with a Best Seller mind can write Best Sellers."

"I am afraid of losing my obscurity. Genuineness only thrives in the dark. Like celery."

Stanley Kubrick, *American director, producer and screenwriter, born Jul 26, 1928*
"If you can talk brilliantly about a problem, it can create the consoling illusion that it has been mastered."

"Mick" (Michael Philip) Jagger, *English musician, born Jul 26, 1943*
"It's all right letting yourself go, as long as you can let yourself back."

JULY 27

Diplomats' Day

First United States cabinet department, Department of Foreign Affairs (later Department of State), established Jul 27, 1789.

"A diplomat is one who can tell a man he's open-minded when he means he has a hole in his head."—*Anon.*

"Diplomacy is the art of saying 'Nice doggie' until you can find a rock."—*Will Rogers*

Alexandre Dumas (Jr.) *French novelist and playwright, born Jul 27, 1824*

"The chain of wedlock is so heavy that it takes two to carry it—sometimes three."

(Joseph-Pierre) Hilaire Belloc, *English poet, essayist, historian, novelist and politician, born Jul 27, 1870*

"I always like to associate with a lot of priests because it makes me understand anti-clerical things so well."

"I'm tired of Love,
I'm still more tired of Rhyme,
But money gives me pleasure all the time."

"When I am dead I hope it may be said
'His sins were scarlet, but his books were read.' "

Leo (Ernest) Durocher, *American baseball player and manager, born Jul 27, 1906*

"Baseball is like church. Many attend. Few understand."

(Lord) Samuel Mancroft, *English essayist, business executive and politician, born Jul 27, 1914*

"Happy the man with a wife to tell him what to do and a secretary to do it for him."

"A speech is like a love affair. Any fool can start it, but to end it requires considerable skill."

JULY 28

Men's Day

"Men should come with instructions."—*Anon.*

"Men have more problems than women. In the first place, they have to put up with women."—*Anon.*

A man asked the clerk in the bookstore, "Have you a book entitled *Man, Master of the Home?*" The clerk looked at him for a moment and then replied, "Try the fiction department, please."

JULY 29

"Don" (Donald Robert Perry) Marquis, *American journalist, poet and playwright, born Jul 29, 1878*

> "Alas! The hours we waste in work
> And similar inconsequence
> Friends, I beg you do not shirk
> Your daily task of indolence."

"There is nothing so habit-forming as money."

"An idea isn't responsible for the people who believe in it."

Benito (Amilcare Andrea) Mussolini, *Italian Fascist dictator, born Jul 29, 1883*

"The history of saints is mainly the history of insane people."

Dag (Hjalmar Agne Carl) Hammarskjöld, *Swedish economist and United Nations Secretary-General, born Jul 29, 1905*

"Time goes by: reputation increases, ability declines."

Melvin (Mouron) Belli, *American lawyer and writer, born Jul 29, 1907*

"I'm not an ambulance chaser. I'm usually there before the ambulance."

JULY 30

Thorstein (Bunde) Veblen, *American economist and social scientist, born Jul 30, 1857*

"Conspicuous consumption of valuable goods is a means of reputability to the gentleman of leisure."

Henry Ford, *American industrialist and automobile pioneer, born Jul 30, 1863*

"An idealist is a person who helps other people to be prosperous."

"History is bunk."

"Exercise is bunk. If you are healthy you don't need it, if you are sick you shouldn't take it."

Lawyer, politician and businessman Chauncey Depew advised his nephew not to invest in Henry Ford's new enterprise. Said he: "Nothing has come along that can beat the horse and buggy."

C(yril) Northcote Parkinson, *English journalist, historian and writer, born Jul 30, 1909*

"We know how to make our predecessors retire. When it comes to forcing us to retire our successors must find some method of their own."

"It is not the business of the botanist to eradicate the weeds. Enough for him if he can just tell us how fast they grow."

Thomas Sowell, *American economist and writer, born Jul 30, 1930*
"There are only two ways of telling the complete truth—anonymously and posthumously."

JULY 31

Advice Day

"Dineros, no consejos" (Spanish saying). [Give me] money, not advice.

"Advice after injury is like medicine after death."—*Danish proverb*

"In love and war, don't seek counsel."—*French proverb*

"If three people say you are an ass, put on a bridle."—*Spanish proverb*

On leaving his post as Montgomery County (Maryland) Executive, James Gleason gave this advice: When leaving office, give your successor three sealed envelopes and instructions to open them, in order, as crises occur in the new administration. Insert these messages: in the first, "blame it on your predecessor"; in the second, "announce a major reorganization"; and in the third, "write out three envelopes for your successor."

August

Beat the Heat Month

Beat the Heat Month

Women are more sensitive to extreme heat, and less sensitive to extreme cold, than men are. (Ladies, keep your cool this summer so you can warm up your man this winter.)

"FLOATING" HOLIDAYS THIS MONTH

Psychic Week first week, Sunday thru Saturday
"I went to a psychic once. He told me I was going to lose a small sum of money. He was right—before I left, he stole my wallet."
—*Eileen Mason*

Umpire Appreciation Week first week, Sunday thru Saturday

Umpire Appreciation Day Saturday of Umpire Appreciation Week

National Smile Week first week, Monday thru Sunday

"To make a smile come, so they say,
brings thirteen muscles into play,
while if you want a frown to thrive,
you've got to work up sixty-five."—*Anon.*

National Family Reunion Day first Sunday
"Nothing spoils a family reunion like those relatives who have managed to stay young-looking and get rich at the same time."—*Anon.*

"Rich relatives are the kin we love to touch."—*Anon.*

AUGUST 1

National Clown Week August 1-7

Hoteliers' Day
"The guest is always right—even if we have to throw him out."
—*Charles (Cesar) Ritz, French hotel executive and restaurateur, born Aug 1, 1891*

"A luxury resort is a place with tropical plants outside, and outstretched palms inside."—*Anon.*

"The great advantage of a hotel is that it is a refuge from home life."—*George Bernard Shaw*

Coulson Kernahan, *English poet, novelist, essayist and critic, born Aug 1, 1858*
"There are two literary maladies—writer's cramp and swelled head. The worst of writer's cramp is that it is never cured; the worst of swelled head is that it never kills."

(Dame Emilie) Rose Macaulay, *English novelist and writer, born Aug 1, 1881*
"It was a book to kill time for those who like it better dead."

"Jerry" (Jerome John) Garcia, *American singer and musician, born Aug 1, 1942*
"Truth is something you stumble into when you think you're going someplace else."

AUGUST 2

John (French) Sloan, *American painter and illustrator, born Aug 2, 1871*
"Since we have to speak well of the dead, let's knock them while they're alive."

James (Arthur) Baldwin, *American novelist, essayist and playwright, born Aug 2, 1924*
"Money, it turned out, was exactly like sex; you thought of nothing else if you didn't have it and thought of other things if you did."

AUGUST 3

Dolores Del Rio, *Mexican actress, born Delores Ansunsolo, Aug 3, 1905*
"Nevair, nevair, will I make a talkie. I zink zey are tairrible."

Richard (Douglas) Lamm, *American lawyer, accountant and politician, born Aug 3, 1935*
"Christmas is a time when kids tell Santa what they want and adults pay for it. Deficits are when adults tell the government what they want—and their kids pay for it."

AUGUST 4

Oscar Ameringer, *American editor, publisher, writer, musician, painter and Socialist party leader, born Aug 4, 1870*
"Politics is the gentle art of getting votes from the poor and campaign funds from the rich, by promising to protect each from the other."

AUGUST 5

Hugh S(amuel) Johnson, *American army officer, journalist and government administrator, born Aug 5, 1882*
"The nearest thing to immortality in this world is a government bureau."

John Huston, *American screenwriter, actor and director, born Aug 5, 1906*
"You need about twenty million dollars to live properly. My life span would probably be lengthened if I had that much. It's only trying to *make* twenty million dollars that cuts short a man's years. Spending it would be healthy."

J(oseph) Clifford Groff, *American (unemployed), born Aug 5, 1960*
"A sales job is easy. I just keep reminding myself these are not really people—they're only customers."

AUGUST 6

(Lord) Alfred Tennyson, *English poet, born Aug 6, 1809*
When Alfred Tennyson was a child, his grandfather paid him ten shillings for writing an elegy on his grandmother, saying: "There, that's the first money you ever earned by your poetry, and take my word for it, it will be the last."

Louella Parsons, *American gossip columnist, born Aug 6, 1881*
"Louella is stronger than Samson. He needed two columns to bring the house down. Louella can do it with one."—*Samuel Goldwyn about Louella Parsons*

Lucille (Désirée) Ball, *American actress and comedienne, born Aug 6, 1911*
"The secret of staying young is to live honestly, eat slowly, sleep sufficiently, work industriously, worship faithfully—and then lie about your age."

Robert Mitchum, *American actor, born Aug 6, 1917*
"I've never been an actor—and I've got seventy movies to prove it."

Andy Warhol, *American painter, sculptor, magazine publisher, film-maker and writer, born Andrew Warhola, Aug 6, 1927*
"I am a deeply superficial person."

AUGUST 7

Share a Secret Day
Mata Hari, *Dutch dancer, courtesan and spy, born Margaretha Geertruida Zelle, Aug 7, 1876*

"If you can't get people to listen to you any other way, tell them it's confidential."—*Farmer's Digest*

"Women can keep secrets as well as men, but it takes more of them to do it."—*Anon.*

AUGUST 8

Politicians' Day
"What's the difference between horse racing and politics? In horse racing the whole horse wins."—*Anon.*

Mario Procaccino, Democratic candidate for Mayor of New York, in 1969 told an audience of black voters, "My heart is as black as yours."

"Politicians make strange bedfellows, but they all share the same bunk."—*Edgar A. Shoaff (biographical information not available)*

Politicians' Day

"Those who are too smart to engage in politics are punished by being governed by those who are dumber."—*Plato, Greek philosopher*

"To err is human; to blame it on the other party is politics."—*Anon.*

"A politician is a man who divides his time between running for office and running for cover."—*Anon.*

"Conservatives are satisfied with present evils; liberals want to replace them with new ones."—*Anon.*

"A conservative is a man who wants the rules changed so that no one can make a pile the way he did."—*Gregory Nunn (biographical information not available)*

AUGUST 9

Gaming Day
"When a man says it's a silly, childish game, it's probably something his wife can beat him at."—*Don Epperson, American actor, born 1938 (birth date not available)*

"Once the game is over, the king and the pawn go back in the same box."—*Italian proverb*

"Victory goes to the player who makes the next-to-last mistake."
—*Savielly Grigorievitch Tartakower, Russian chess player, born 1887 (birth date not available)*

"It is not enough to aim, you must hit."—*Italian proverb*

Robert Aldrich, *American director and producer, born Aug 9, 1918*
"A director is a ringmaster, a psychiatrist, and a referee."

AUGUST 10

Horace Fletcher, *American nutritionist and writer, born Aug 10, 1849*
"Nature will castigate those who don't masticate."

Herbert (Clark) Hoover, *American engineer, politician and 31st US President, born Aug 10, 1874*
"Blessed are the young, for they shall inherit the national debt."

He was the first president born west of the Mississippi and the first to have a telephone on his desk.

Louis Sobol, *American journalist, born Aug 10, 1896*
"Some of the songs making the rounds now will be popular when Bach, Beethoven, and Wagner are forgotten—but not before."

AUGUST 11

Experts' Day/Consultants' Day
"An expert is a person who can take something you already know and make it sound confusing."—*Anon.*

"The word 'expert' derives from 'ex,' a has-been, and 'spurt,' a drip under pressure."—*Anon.*

"Expert: someone who knows more and more about less and less."
—*Anon.*

"A consultant is someone who takes your watch away to tell you what time it is."—*Ed Finkelstein (biographical information not available)*

AUGUST 12

(Baroness) Norah Phillips, *English lady in waiting to Her Majesty Queen Elizabeth II, born Aug 12, 1910*
"I liked the store detective who said he'd seen a lot of people who were so confused that they'd stolen things, but never one so confused that they'd paid twice."

George Hamilton, *American actor, born Aug 12, 1939*
"The hard thing is to be married with style. Being single is a breeze. Nowadays, you can have a head-on collision on Sunset Boulevard and end up going home with the girl you hit."

AUGUST 13

International Lefthanders Day
"If the right side of the brain controls the left side of the body, then only left-handed people are in their right minds."—*Anon.*

Bert Lahr, *American actor and comedian, born Irving Lahrheim Aug 13, 1895*
"Hollywood is the only community in the world where the entire population is suffering from rumortism."

(Sir) Alfred (Joseph) Hitchcock, *English director, born Aug 13, 1899*
"Hitchcock uses a lot of skill over a lot of nothing."—*James Agee about Alfred Hitchcock*

"The best screen actor is the man who can do nothing extremely well."

"The length of a film should be directly related to the endurance of the human bladder."

"Television has brought murder back into the home—where it belongs."

AUGUST 14

John Galsworthy, *English novelist and playwright, born Aug 14, 1867*
"Idealism increases in direct proportion to one's distance from the problem."

Russell (Wayne) Baker, *American journalist and writer, born Aug 14, 1925*
"Inanimate objects are classified scientifically into three major categories—those that don't work, those that break down, and those that get lost."

"Don't try to make children grow up to be like you, or they may do it."

Mark Stevens, *American novelist, writer and art critic, born Aug 14, 1951*
On a celebrity restaurant: "They serve you your importance."

AUGUST 15

National Relaxation Day
(Be like an accountant. Don't do anything too taxing.)

Napoleon Bonaparte, *French emperor, born Aug 15, 1769*
"Glory is fleeting, but obscurity is forever."

"What is history but a fable agreed upon?"

"Give me a man with a good allowance of nose.... When I want any good headwork done, I always choose a man, if suitable otherwise, with a long nose."

"The only victory over love is flight."

"My downfall raises me to infinite heights."

(Sir) Walter Scott, *Scottish novelist, poet, historian and biographer, born Aug 15, 1771*
"I care not who knows it—I write for the general amusement."

Ethel Barrymore, *American actress, born Ethel Blythe, Aug 15, 1879*
"You grow up the day you have your first real laugh—at yourself."

Edna Ferber, *American novelist and playwright, born Aug 15, 1887*
"A woman can look both moral and exciting—if she also looks as if it were quite a struggle."

Lillian Carter, *mother of 39th US President, born Aug 15, 1898*
"Sometimes when I look at my children I say to myself, 'Lillian, you should have stayed a virgin.'"

Julia Child, *American cookbook writer and television personality, born Aug 15, 1912*
"The only real stumbling block is fear of failure. In cooking you've got to have a what-the-hell attitude."

Robert F(rancis) Goheen, *American educator, born Aug 15, 1919*
"If you feel that you have both feet planted on the ground then the university has failed you."

Phyllis (Stewart) Schlafly, *American lawyer, columnist, antifeminist and writer, born Aug 15, 1924*
"Phyllis Schlafly should be tied up and forced to watch people minding their own business."—*Elayne Boosler about Phyllis Schlafly*

"Phyllis Schlafly speaks for all American women who oppose equal rights for themselves."—*Andy Rooney about Phyllis Schlafly*

Princess Anne (Elizabeth Alice Louise), *English royalty (daughter of Queen Elizabeth II), born Aug 15, 1950*
"When I appear in public people expect me to neigh, grind my teeth, paw the ground and swish my tail—none of which is easy."

AUGUST 16

(Jean de) La Bruyère, *French writer, philosopher and satirist, born Aug 16, 1645*
"Next to sound judgment, diamonds and pearls are the rarest things in the world."

Bernarr (Adolphus) Macfadden, *American publisher, born Bernard Adolphus Macfadden, Aug 16, 1868*
It's a *True Story*. He made a parachute jump over Paris at age 84.

Charles (Henry) Bukowski (Jr.), *American editor, short-story writer, novelist and poet, born Aug 16, 1920*
"A whore is a woman who takes more than she gives. A man who takes more than he gives is called a businessman."

AUGUST 17

Mae Day

Mae West, *American actress, born Aug 17, 1892*
"A curved line is the loveliest distance between two points."

"You're never too old to become younger."

"She's the kind of girl who climbed the ladder of success, wrong by wrong."

"Brains are an asset, if you hide them."

"He's the kind of man a woman would have to marry to get rid of."

"Marriage is a great institution, but I'm not ready for an institution."

"To catch a husband is an art; to hold him is a job."

"When women go wrong, men go right after them."

"I go for two kinds of men. The kind with muscles, and the kind without."

"Fifty men outside? I'm tired. Send ten of them home."

"He who hesitates is a damned fool."

"The man I don't like doesn't exist."

"Love conquers all things except poverty and toothache."

"It takes two to make trouble for one."

"Goodness had nothing to do with it, honey."

"When choosing between two evils, I always like to take the one I've never tried before."

"I only like two kinds of men: domestic and foreign."

"It's not the men in my life that counts—it's the life in my men."

"Can I cook? Nobody ever asked me to."

"Honey, I'm single because I was born that way. I never married, because I would have had to give up my favorite hobby—men."

"With apologies to Shakespeare, some are born sexy, others become sexy, and some, like myself, have sexiness thrust upon them."

"I've been in more laps than a napkin."

AUGUST 18

Shelley Winters, *American actress, born Shirley Schrift, Aug 18, 1922*
"In Hollywood, all marriages are happy. It's trying to live together afterward that causes the problems."

"Now that I'm over sixty I'm veering toward respectability."

"It was so cold I almost got married."

"Weight is only a state of mind. To me, anyone under 150 pounds is just bones with a slip-cover on."

(Charles) Robert Redford (Jr.), *American actor, born Aug 18, 1937*
"If you stay in Beverly Hills too long you become a Mercedes."

AUGUST 19

National Aviation Day
    Orville Wright, *American inventor and aviation pioneer, born Aug 19, 1871.*

    "Pilots are just plane people with a special air about them."—*Anon.*

In 1954 the mayor of the Châteauneuf-du-Pape community in France passed a law banning all flying saucers from landing in the area.

John Dryden, *English poet, playwright and critic, born Aug 19, 1631*
"Beware the fury of a patient man."

Bernard (Mannes) Baruch, *American financier, statesman and writer, born Aug 19, 1870*
"Vote for the man who promises least; he'll be the least disappointing."

Ogden (Frederic) Nash, *American poet, born Aug 19, 1902*
"You only tease the things you love."

    "There is one fault that I must find
    With the twentieth century,
    And I'll put it in a couple of words:
    Too adventury.
    What I'd like would be some nice dull monotony
    If anyone's gotony."

    "There is only one way to achieve happiness on this terrestrial ball, and that is to have either a clear conscience or none at all."

    "There are two kinds of people who blow through life like a breeze. And one kind is gossipers, and the other kind is gossipees."

"Senescence begins
And middle age ends,
The day your descendants
Outnumber your friends."

"He without benefit of scruples
His fun and money soon quadruples."

"Undeniably brash
Was young Ogden Nash,
Whose notable verse
Was admirably terse
And written with panache."

"Do you think my mind is maturing late
Or simply rotted early?"

Malcolm S(tevenson) Forbes, *American publisher, editor and sportsman, born Aug 19, 1919*
"Men who never get carried away should be."

"When in doubt, duck."

"There is never enough time, unless you're serving it."

"By the time we've made it, we've had it."

Richard (Reid) Ingrams, *English journalist, editor and satirist, born Aug 19, 1937*
"I have come to regard the Law Courts not as a cathedral, but as a casino."

AUGUST 20

Edgar A(lbert) Guest, *American poet and journalist, born Aug 20, 1881*
"When turkey's on the table laid,
And good things I may scan,
I'm thankful that I wasn't made
A vegetarian."

L(eonard) Binder, *American historian, born Aug 20, 1927*
"Confidence is simply that quiet assured feeling you have before you fall flat on your face."

AUGUST 21

Lawyers' Day
American Bar Association organized Aug 21, 1878

Lawyers' Day

"Whene'er a bitter foe attack thee
Sheathe thy sword, thy wrath restrain;
Or else will magistrates and lawyers
Divide thy wealth, thy purse retain."—*Archevolti (16th century)*

"A lawyer is a man who advises his clients how not to lose all they own to anyone but him."—*Anon.*

"A chi consiglia, no duole il capo" (Italian saying). He who gives the counsel doesn't get the headaches.

"If you still believe talk is cheap, you haven't hired a lawyer."
    —*Anon.*

"When an irresistible force meets an immovable object, there's usually a lawyer who will take the case."—*Anon.*

"It is the trade of lawyers to question everything, yield nothing, and talk by the hour."—*Anon.*

"Of three things the devil makes a stew: lawyers' tongues, lovers' promises, and ungrateful children."—*Italian proverb*

"It is better to be a mouse in a cat's mouth than a man in a lawyer's hands."—*Spanish proverb*

Peter (David) Anderson, *American lawyer, born Aug 21, 1940*
"Stealing someone else's words frequently spares the embarrassment of eating your own."

AUGUST 22

Dorothy Parker, *American poet, short-story writer and critic, born Dorothy Rothschild, Aug 22, 1893*
"By the time you say you're his,
Shivering and sighing
And he vows his passion is
Infinite, undying—
Lady, make a note of this:
One of you is lying."

"The best way to keep children home is to make the home a pleasant atmosphere—and let the air out of the tires."

"Brevity is the soul of lingerie."

"An anthologist is a lazy fellow who likes to spend a quiet evening at home raiding good books."

"Razors pain you;
Rivers are damp;
Acids stain you;
And drugs cause cramp.
Guns aren't lawful;
Nooses give;
Gas smells awful;
You might as well live."

"Women and elephants never forget."

"This is not a novel to be tossed aside lightly. It should be thrown with great force."

"I don't care what is written about me so long as it isn't true."

"I was following in the exquisite footsteps of Miss Edna St. Vincent Millay, unhappily in my own horrible sneakers."

AUGUST 23

"Gene" (Eugene Curran) Kelly, *American dancer, director and actor, born Aug 23, 1912*
"The joy of my kind of dancing is that you never forget it's an eternal fertility rite."

Mark Russell, *American comedian, born Mark Ruslander,*
Aug 23, 1932
"The scientific theory I like best is that the rings of Saturn are composed entirely of lost airline luggage."

Pete (Barton) Wilson, *American educator and politician, born*
Aug 23, 1933
His administration as mayor of San Diego was once described as "the bland leading the bland."

AUGUST 24

"Max" (Sir Henry Maximilian) Beerbohm, *English writer, critic and caricaturist, born Aug 24, 1872*
"Only the insane take themselves quite seriously."

"There is always something absurd about the past."

"Most women are not so young as they are painted."

"It distresses me, this failure to keep pace with the leaders of thought, as they pass into oblivion."

Malcolm Cowley, *American social historian, editor, poet and critic, born Aug 24, 1898*
"They tell you that you'll lose your mind when you grow older. What they don't tell you is that you won't miss it very much."

Jorge Luis Borges, *Argentine poet, short-story writer and critic, born Aug 24, 1899*
"My father and he had one of those English friendships which begin by avoiding intimacies and eventually eliminate speech altogether."

"Every writer creates his own precursors."

"The past is always being changed."

AUGUST 25

Detectives' Day
  Allan Pinkerton, *American detective-agency founder, born Aug 25, 1819*
Founded in 1812 by detective François Vidocq, France's famed Sureté was originally staffed entirely with ex-convicts.

A "clue" originally meant a ball of thread, hence the expression "to unravel" a mystery.

Bret Harte, *American poet, novelist and journalist, born Francis Brett Harte, Aug 25, 1836*
"One big vice in a man is apt to keep out a great many smaller ones."

William Feather, *American publisher, essayist and journalist, born Aug 25, 1889*

> "Setting a good example for your children takes all the fun out of middle age."

Leonard Bernstein, *American conductor and composer, born Aug 25, 1918*

> Leonard Bernstein's father actively and continually discouraged his son's interest in music and tried to get him to go into the family's beauty supply business instead. When asked about this some years later, the elder Bernstein responded, "How was I to know he was *Leonard Bernstein?*"

AUGUST 26

Women's Equality Day

> 19th Amendment to United States Constitution, prohibiting discrimination on the basis of sex with regard to voting, ratified Aug 26, 1920.

> In 1905, former President Grover Cleveland wrote in the *Ladies' Home Journal*, "Sensible and responsible women do not want to vote."

> "Life isn't fair to us men. When we are born, our mothers get the compliments and the flowers. When we are married, our brides get the presents and the publicity. When we die, our widows get the life insurance and winters in Florida. What do women want to be liberated from?"—*Anon.*

> In the mid-1970's Irish officials advertised for an Enforcement Officer to implement regulations mandating equal pay for both sexes. The ad specified different salaries for men and women.

Earl Derr Biggers, *American columnist, novelist and playwright, born Aug 26, 1884*

> "Roundabout way often shortest way to correct destination."
> —*Charlie Chan, character created by Earl Derr Biggers*

Christopher (William Bradshaw-)Isherwood, *American novelist and playwright, born Aug 26, 1904*

> "A screenwriter is a man who is being tortured to confess and has nothing to confess."

AUGUST 27

Samuel Goldwyn, *American producer, born Samuel Goldfish Aug 27, 1882*

> "You always knew where you stood with Sam Goldwyn: nowhere."—*F. Scott Fitzgerald about Samuel Goldwyn*

"Sam Goldwyn was his own greatest production."—*Richard Schickel about Samuel Goldwyn*

"A verbal contract isn't worth the paper it's written on."

"Don't let your opinion sway your judgment."

"I'll give you a definite maybe."

"I'm exhausted from not talking."

"The most important thing in acting is *honesty*; once you learn to fake that, you're in!"

"Too caustic? To hell with the cost, we'll make the picture anyway."

"I had a monumental idea this morning, but I didn't like it."

"Anyone who goes to a psychiatrist ought to have his head examined."

"Don't pay any attention to the critics—don't even ignore them."

"All the lies they tell about me are true."

"The trouble with this business is the dearth of bad pictures."

"Television has raised writing to a new low."

" 'The directorial skill of Mamoulian, the radiance of Anna Sten and the genius of Goldwyn have united to make the world's greatest entertainment.' That is the kind of ad I like. Facts. No exaggeration."

"I don't want any yes-men around me. I want everybody to tell me the truth even if it costs them their jobs."

Lyndon Baines Johnson, *American teacher, politician and 36th US President, born Aug 27, 1908*

"Only two things are necessary to keep one's wife happy. One is to let her think she is having her own way, and the other, to let her have it."

"Frank" (Francis William) Leahy, *American football coach, born Aug 27, 1908*

"Egotism is the anesthetic that dulls the pain of stupidity."

AUGUST 28

Check Your Radar Day

First jail sentence for speeding handed out in Newport, Rhode Island, Aug 28, 1904.

"The trouble with life in the fast lane is that you get to the end in an awful hurry."—*Anon.*

Johann Wolfgang von Goethe, *German poet, novelist, playwright and philosopher, born Aug 28, 1749*

"One never goes so far as when one doesn't know where one is going."

"To disavow an error is to invent retroactively."

"Love is an ideal thing, marriage a real thing; a confusion of the real with the ideal never goes unpunished."

"If children grew up according to early indications, we should have nothing but geniuses."

"To measure up to all that is demanded of him, a man must overestimate his capacities."

"A clever man commits no minor blunders."

"When ideas fail, words come in very handy."

"Know thyself? If I knew myself, I'd run away."

He wrote his first play when he was 10, and before he entered the university at 16, he had learned Latin, Greek, French, Italian, and English.

C(harles) Wright Mills, *American teacher and sociologist, born Aug 28, 1916*
"Nobody talks more of free enterprise and competition and of the best man winning than the man who inherited his father's store or farm."

Crandall Condra, *American lawyer, born Aug 28, 1919*
"America's favorite indoor sport used to be sex. Now it's litigation."

AUGUST 29

Oliver Wendell Holmes (Sr.), *American physician, educator, poet, essayist, novelist and humorist, born Aug 29, 1809*
"Man has his will—but woman has her way."

"The young man knows the rules but the old man knows the exceptions."

"Now when a doctor's patients are perplexed,
A consultation comes in order next—
You know what that is? In a certain place
Meet certain doctors to discuss a case
And other matters, such as weather, crops,
Potatoes, pumpkins, lager-beer, and hops."

Charles F(ranklin) Kettering, *American engineer and automobile pioneer, born Aug 29, 1876*
"The difference between intelligence and education is this: intelligence will make you a good living."

Ingrid Bergman, *Swedish actress, born Aug 29, 1915*
"Happiness is good health and a bad memory."

AUGUST 30

Chef's Day
In a recipe: "If they like it, it serves four; otherwise, six."
—*Elsie Zussman (biographical information not available)*

"The feminist movement has helped open minds and kitchens to the notion that men can be at home on the range."—*René Veaux, French chef (birth date not available)*

"Be content to remember that those who can make omelettes properly can do nothing else."—*Hilaire Belloc*

AUGUST 31

Find a Tax Haven Day
"The two leading recipes for success are building a better mousetrap and finding a bigger loophole."—*Edgar A. Shoaff (biographical information not available)*

"A hypocrite is a man who pays his taxes with a smile."—*Anon.*

"Behind every successful man stands a woman and the IRS. One takes the credit, and the other takes the cash."—*Anon.*

"If Patrick Henry thought that taxation without representation was bad, he should see how bad it is with representation."—*The Old Farmer's Almanac*

Virgil, the Roman poet, once held a funeral for a fly, including pallbearers and eulogies, and buried it on the land surrounding his private villa. Why? In ancient Rome, cemetery land was not taxable. (Was that a tax haven or a tax heaven?)

Arthur Godfrey, *American actor and radio/television host, born Aug 31, 1903*
"I'm proud to be paying taxes in the US. The only thing is—I could be just as proud for half the money."

"When I'm seventy, I want to be named in a paternity suit."

September

National Clock Month

The most widely quoted poem in the English language is the one that begins, "Thirty days hath September," by Richard Grafton.

"Thirty-one days hath July
Tho' no one's been able to figure out why.
And poor February's the shortest month in the race
E'en when it 'leaps' to a day-longer space.

But thanks, Richard Grafton—we'll never forget
Thirty days hath September—and it's not over yet."—*Eileen Mason*

National Clock Month
"What is time? If I am not asked, I know; if I am asked, I don't."
—*St. Augustine*

"Time is nature's way of keeping everything from happening
at once."—*Anon.*

"There was a young lady named Bright
Who could travel much faster than light
She started one day
In the relative way
And came back on the previous night."—*Anon.*

"If you want everything done yesterday, what will you do
tomorrow?"—*Anon.*

Be Kind to Editors and Writers Month
"Some editors are failed writers, but so are most writers."—*T.S. Eliot*

"FLOATING" HOLIDAYS THIS MONTH

National Singles Week Sunday thru Saturday, beginning third
Sunday

Banned Books Week Saturday thru Saturday, beginning fourth
Saturday

National Food Service Employees Week fourth week, Sunday
thru Saturday

National Food Service Employees Day Wednesday of National
Food Service Employees Week

"We wish you health, dear waitress—
And may you be preserved
From accident or illness—
At least till we've been served."—*Anon.*

Capital Day observed in United States Saturday before Labor Day
(honoring savers and investors)

"Saving is a very fine thing. Especially when your parents have
done it for you."—*Winston Churchill*

"First secure an independent income, then practice virtue."
—*Greek saying*

Labor Day observed in United States first Monday
"If all the cars in the United States were placed end to end, it would
probably be Labor Day Weekend."—*Doug Larson (biographical
information not available)*

"Too many people quit looking for work when they find a job."
—*Anon.*

"The trouble with unemployment is that the minute you wake up in the morning you're on the job."—*Slappy White, American comedian (birth date not available)*

"The thing that really worries business today is the great number of people still on their payroll who are unemployed."—*Anon.*

"You can tell a British workman by his hands. They are always in his pockets."—*Anon.*

"The closest most people come to perfection is when they fill out a job application."—*Anon.*

"To me a job is an invasion of privacy."—*Danny McGoorty, American pool player, born 1901 (birth date not available)*

"When I realized that what I had turned out to be was a lousy, two-bit hustler and drunk, I wasn't depressed at all. I was glad to have a profession."—*Danny McGoorty*

> "Too much work and no vacation
> Deserves at least a small libation—
> So hail your friends and raise your glasses;
> Work's the curse of the drinking classes."—*Anon.*

National Grandparents Day   observed in United States Sunday following Labor Day
> "Perfect love sometimes does not come till the first grandchild."
> —*Welsh proverb*

International Day of Peace   third Tuesday
> (sponsored by United Nations on opening day of regular session of General Assembly)

> "When two elephants fight, it is the grass that gets trampled."
> —*Swahili proverb*

> *"Cu'e orbu, bordu e taci campa cent'anni 'n paci"* (Sicilian saying).
> He who is deaf, dumb and blind will live a hundred years in peace.

National Good Neighbor Day   fourth Sunday
> "When you think of all the lonely people without relatives or neighbors, you certainly envy them."—*Anon.*

> Neighbor: "One whom we are commanded to love as ourselves, and who does all he knows how to make us disobedient."—*Ambrose Bierce*

National Hunting and Fishing Day   fourth Saturday
> "A canny young fisher named Fisher
> Once fished on the edge of a fissure
> A fish with a grin
> Pulled the fisherman in—
> Now they're fishing the fissure for Fisher."—*Anon.*

"Old hunters never quit; they just change their game."—*Anon.*

"Some fishermen catch their best fish by the tale."—*Anon.*

Autumnal Equinox in Northern Hemisphere (Fall begins) about
Sep 22
"Fall is my favorite season in Los Angeles, watching the birds
change color and fall from the trees."—*David Letterman*

SEPTEMBER 1

James Gordon Bennett, *American newspaper publisher, born
Sep 1, 1795*
"So many a good story is ruined by overreliance on truth."

"Kin" (Frank McKinney) Hubbard, *American journalist,
caricaturist, cartoonist and humorist, born Sep 1, 1868*
"Distant relatives er th' best kind, an' th' further th' better."

"The safe way to double your money is to fold it over once and
put it in your pocket."

"It's going to be fun to watch and see how long the meek can keep
the earth after they inherit it."

"I'll say this for adversity—people seem to be able to stand it, and
that's more'n I kin say fer prosperity."

"Justice: a system of revenge where the state imitates the criminal."

"Nobody ever forgets where he buried the hatchet."

Lily Tomlin, *American comedienne and actress, born Sep 1, 1939*
"Ninety-eight percent of the adults in this country are decent, hard-
working, honest Americans. It's the other lousy two percent that
get all the publicity. But then—we elected them."

"If truth is beauty, how come no one has their hair done in
the library?"

"If love is the answer, could you rephrase the question?"

SEPTEMBER 2

Numismatists' Day
United States Treasury Department established by Congress
Sep 2, 1789.

"If you want to know what God thinks about money, look at some of
the people He gives it to."—*Anon.*

"I can't take it with me I know
But will it last until I go?"—*Martha F. Newmeyer (biographical
information not available)*

"He's so generous he'd give you the sleeves out of his vest."—*Anon.*

"How little you know about the age you live in if you think that honey is sweeter than cash in hand."—*Ovid, Roman poet*

"Money may not buy happiness. But with it you can rent enough."—*Anon.*

"Remember the Golden Rule: He who has the gold makes the rules."—*Anon.*

Cleveland Amory, *American radio/television journalist, editor, writer and champion of animal causes, born Sep 2, 1917*
"Opera is like a husband with a foreign title: expensive to support, hard to understand, and therefore a supreme social challenge."

SEPTEMBER 3

Kitty Carlisle, *American actress and singer, born Catherine Holzman, Sep 3, 1915*
"TV cameras seem to add ten pounds to me. So I make it a policy never to eat TV cameras."

SEPTEMBER 4

Newspaper Carriers' Day
First "newsboy," ten-year-old Barney Flaherty, hired in United States Sep 4, 1833.

Photographers' Day
George Eastman patented the first roll-film camera and registered the name Kodak Sep 4, 1888.

"You can't depend on your eyes when your imagination is out of focus."—*Mark Twain*

Paul Harvey, *American columnist and broadcast journalist, born Paul Harvey Aurandt, Sep 4, 1918*
"Fathers are what give daughters away to other men who aren't nearly good enough, so they can have grandchildren who are smarter than anybody's."

SEPTEMBER 5

Be Late for Something Day

Darryl F(rancis) Zanuck, *American producer and film executive, born Sep 5, 1902*
"For God's sake, don't say yes until I've finished talking."

"Whenever the publicity department calls me a genius, I always remind them of the time I refused to sign Gable because I thought his ears were too big."

John (Milton) Cage (Jr.), *American composer, teacher, writer and poet, born Sep 5, 1912*
"I have nothing to say and I'm saying it and that is poetry."

SEPTEMBER 6

Look Up That Old Gang of Yours Day
Billy Rose, *American songwriter and theatrical producer, born William Samuel Rosenberg, Sep 6, 1899*

Eccentrics' Day
Eccentrics live longer than more traditional people, according to a study reported in *Longevity*. Possible reasons: purpose in life, strong sense of self, love of ideas, sense of humor. For a long life, get weird!

SEPTEMBER 7

Grandma Moses, *American folk painter, born Anna Mary Robertson, Sep 7, 1860*
"If I didn't start painting, I would have raised chickens."

(Dame) Edith Sitwell, *English poet, writer and critic, born Sep 7, 1887*
"Good taste is the worst vice ever invented."

"I am debarred from putting her in her place—she hasn't got one."

"I have often wished I had time to cultivate modesty.... But I am too busy thinking about myself."

Ivy (Maude) Baker Priest, *American government official, politician and US Treasurer, born Sep 7, 1905*
"We women don't care too much about getting our pictures on money as long as we can get our hands on it."

SEPTEMBER 8

International Literacy Day
"A book is a mirror: When a monkey looks in, no apostle can look out."—*Anon.*

Howard Dietz, *American lyricist and film executive, born Sep 8, 1896*
  "Composers shouldn't think too much—it interferes with
  their plagiarism."

Denise Darcel, *American actress and singer, born Sep 8, 1925*
  "Hollywood is no place for a woman to find a husband, especially
  her own."

SEPTEMBER 9

(Cardinal) Armand Jean du Plessis, duc de Richelieu, *French
clergyman and statesman, born Sep 9, 1585*
  "Give me six lines written by the most honorable of men and I will
  find an excuse in them to hang him."

(Count) Leo (Lev Nikolayevich) Tolstoy, *Russian novelist, short-
story writer, playwright and philosopher, born Sep 9, 1828*
  "Historians are like deaf people who go on answering questions that
  no one has asked them."

  "He who has money has in his pocket those who have none."

Granville Hicks, *American novelist, critic and teacher, born Sep 9, 1901*
  "A censor is a man who knows more than he thinks you ought to."

Joseph E(dward) Levine, *American producer, born Sep 9, 1905*
  "You can fool all the people all of the time if the advertising is right
  and the budget is big enough."

Cesare Pavese, *Italian poet, short-story writer, novelist, translator,
editor and critic, born Sep 9, 1908*
  "No woman marries for money: they are all clever enough, before
  marrying a millionaire, to fall in love with him first."

Sylvia Miles, *American actress and comedienne, born Sep 9, 1932*
  "Sylvia Miles would go to the opening of an envelope."—*Anon.
  about Sylvia Miles*

SEPTEMBER 10

Brainstorming Day/Swap Ideas Day
  "The function of genius is not to give new answers, but pose new
  questions which time and mediocrity can resolve."—*Anon.*

Cyril (Vernon) Connolly, *English critic, editor, novelist and writer,
born Sep 10, 1903*
  "As repressed sadists are said to become policemen or butchers so
  those with an irrational fear of life become publishers."

Brainstorming Day/Swap Ideas Day

"There is no more sombre enemy of good art than the pram in the hall."

"Longevity is the revenge of talent upon genius."

"No one can make us hate ourselves like an admirer."

Charles (Bishop) Kuralt, *American broadcast journalist and writer, born Sep 10, 1934*
  "Thanks to the interstate highway system, it is now possible to travel across the country from coast to coast without seeing anything."

SEPTEMBER 11

O. Henry, *American short-story writer and journalist, born William Sydney Porter, Sep 11, 1862*
  "A straw vote only shows the way the hot air blows."

D(avid) H(erbert) Lawrence, *English novelist, playwright, short-story writer, poet, essayist and critic, born Sep 11, 1885*

"His descriptive powers were remarkable, but his ideas cannot too soon be forgotten."—*Bertrand Russell about D.H. Lawrence*

"It's bad taste to be wise all the time...."

"Tom" (Thomas Wade) Landry, *American football player and coach, born Sep 11, 1924*

"He's a perfectionist. If he was married to Raquel Welch, he'd expect her to cook."—*Don Meredith about Tom Landry*

David (Salzer) Broder, *American journalist and writer, born Sep 11, 1929*

"Anybody that wants the presidency so much that he'll spend two years organizing and campaigning for it is not to be trusted with the office."

SEPTEMBER 12

H(enry) L(ouis) Mencken, *American journalist, editor, critic and writer, born Sep 12, 1880*

"A politician is an animal which can sit on a fence and yet keep both ears to the ground."

"Self-respect—the secure feeling that no one, as yet, is suspicious."

"A society made up of individuals who were all capable of original thought would probably be unendurable."

"Puritanism—The haunting fear that someone, somewhere, may be happy."

"An idealist is one who, on noticing that a rose smells better than a cabbage, concludes that it will also make better soup."

"A prohibitionist is the sort of man one wouldn't care to drink with, even if he drank."

"Bachelors know more about women than married men. If they didn't, they'd be married, too."

"Church is a place in which gentlemen who have never been to heaven brag about it to people who will never get there."

"Love is the triumph of imagination over intelligence."

"It is inaccurate to say I hate everything. I am strongly in favor of common sense, common honesty, and common decency. This makes me forever ineligible for any public office."

"The older I grow the more I distrust the familiar doctrine that age brings wisdom."

"If, after I depart this vale, you ever remember me and have thought to please my ghost, forgive some sinner and wink your eye at some homely girl."

"Injustice is relatively easy to bear; what stings is justice."

His "Happy Formula" for answering controversial letters is final, courteous, and can be used without reading the missive to which it replies: "Dear Sir [or Madame]: You may be right."

On Aug 27, 1930 H.L. Mencken married Sara Powell Haardt, whom he had met while in Maryland to give a lecture on "How to Catch a Husband."

SEPTEMBER 13

Henry F(ountain) Ashurst, *American lawyer and politician, born Sep 13, 1874*
  "Silence is the best substitute for brains ever invented."

Sherwood Anderson, *American novelist, poet and short-story writer, born Sep 13, 1876*
  "The possessor of a brilliant and almost inimitable prose style, and of scarcely any ideas at all."—*F. Scott Fitzgerald about Sherwood Anderson*

Miss Manners (Judith Sylvia Martin), *American journalist, critic and etiquette authority, born Judith Sylvia Perlman, Sep 13, 1938*
  "What you have when everyone wears the same playclothes for all occasions, is addressed by nickname, expected to participate in Show and Tell, and bullied out of any desire for privacy, is not democracy; it is kindergarten."

SEPTEMBER 14

Be Kind to Absent-Minded Professors Day
  In the 1800s, a Dr. Heath at Eton College created what may be a record by whipping seventy boys, one after another. He injured himself so badly that he was laid up with aches and pains for more than a week.

  "A college student is someone who's learned to write home for money in three or four languages."—*Anon.*

  "If nobody dropped out at the eighth grade, who would hire the college graduates?"—*Anon.*

  "A college education seldom hurts a man if he's willing to learn a little something after he graduates."—*Anon.*

  "American college students are like American colleges—each has half-dulled faculties."—*James Thurber*

SEPTEMBER 15

Felt Hat Day (Time to put away the straw and get felt)

(François, duc de) La Rochefoucauld, *French writer, born Sep 15, 1613*
"An old man gives good advice in order to console himself for no longer being in condition to set a bad example."

William Howard Taft, *American jurist, teacher, US Secretary of War, 27th US President and US Supreme Court Justice, born Sep 15, 1857*
"Some men are graduated from college cum laude, some are graduated summa cum laude, and some are graduated mirabile dictu."

Robert (Charles) Benchley, *American actor, writer and humorist, born Sep 15, 1889*
"In America there are two classes of travel—first and with children."

"I must step out of these wet things and into a dry martini."

"A great many people have come up to me and asked how I managed to get so much done and still look so dissipated."

"Most of the arguments to which I am a party fall somewhat short of being impressive owing to the fact that neither I nor my opponent knows what we are talking about."

"Drawing on my fine command of language, I said nothing."

"It was one of those plays in which all the actors unfortunately enunciated very clearly."

"I'm glad this question came up, in a way, because there are so many different ways to answer it that one of them is bound to be right."

"The surest way of making a monkey out of a man is to quote him."

"I am the oldest living man—especially at seven in the morning."

"It took me fifteen years to discover that I had no talent for writing, but I couldn't give it up because by that time I was too famous."

"I do most of my work sitting down. That's where I shine."

(Dame) Agatha (Mary Clarissa) Christie, *English novelist and playwright, born Sep 15, 1890*
"Curious things, habits. People themselves never knew they had them."

"It is completely unimportant. That is why it is so interesting."

"If one sticks too rigidly to one's principles one would hardly see anybody."

"One of the oddest things in life, I think, is the things one remembers."

"An archeologist is the best husband a woman can have; the older she gets, the more interested he is in her." (She was married to one.)

Jean Renoir, *French director, born Sep 15, 1894*
"... it certainly has been a pleasure working at Sixteenth Century-Fox."

Penny Singleton, *American actress, born Dorothy McNulty Sep 15, 1908*
"I'm not as young as my teeth or as old as my tongue."

SEPTEMBER 16

Laurence J(ohnston) Peter, *American teacher, writer and anthologist, born Sep 16, 1919*
"Heredity is what sets the parents of a teenager wondering about each other."

"Education is a method by which one acquires a higher grade of prejudices."

"An economist is an expert who will know tomorrow why the things he predicted yesterday didn't happen today."

"Two liars are company, three are a crowd, and four or more a chamber of commerce."

"Computers will never be perfected until they can compute how much more than the estimate the job will cost."

"Television has changed the American child from an irresistible force into an immovable object."

"Food is a consuming passion."

"Political success is the ability, when the inevitable occurs, to get credit for it."

"Most hierarchies were established by men who now monopolize the upper levels, thus depriving women of their rightful share of opportunities for incompetence."

"Prison will not work until we start sending a better class of people there."

Lauren Bacall, *American actress, born Betty Joan Perske, Sep 16, 1924*
"If goodness is its own reward, shouldn't we get a little something for being naughty?"

"I suppose eighty is the proper time for getting married because then you can be sure it will last."

"I hate parties. Why should I spend my energy decorating somebody's room?"

SEPTEMBER 17

Citizenship Day in United States

Constitution Week in United States Sep 17-23

Proposed United States Constitution approved by delegates to Constitutional Convention Sep 17, 1787.

"A real patriot is someone who gets a parking ticket and rejoices that the system works."—*Anon.*

"Duty: What one expects of others."—*Anon.*

"Ask not what you can do for your country, for they are liable to tell you."—*Mark Steinbeck (biographical information not available)*

SEPTEMBER 18

Samuel Johnson, *English critic, poet, journalist, essayist and lexicographer, born Sep 18, 1709*

"Marriage is the triumph of hope over experience."

"A man is in general better pleased when he has a good dinner upon the table than when his wife talks Greek."

"There is nothing which has yet been contrived by man, by which so much happiness is produced as by a good tavern."

"I found your essay to be good and original. However, the part that was original was not good and the part that was good was not original."

Joseph Story, *American lawyer, teacher and US Supreme Court Justice, born Sep 18, 1779*

"It is astonishing how easily men satisfy themselves that the Constitution is exactly what they wish it to be."

SEPTEMBER 19

(Lord) Henry Peter Brougham, *Scottish jurist and politician, born Sep 19, 1778*

"A lawyer is a learned gentleman who rescues your estate from your enemies and keeps it himself."

"Joe" (Joseph) Pasternak, *Hungarian producer, born Sep 19, 1901*

"You call this a script? Give me a couple of $5,000-a-week writers and I'll write it myself."

SEPTEMBER 20

(Sir) James Dewar, *Scottish physicist and chemist, born Sep 20, 1842*
"Love is an ocean of emotions, entirely surrounded by expenses."

Upton (Beall) Sinclair, *American novelist, born Sep 20, 1878*
"It is difficult to get a man to understand something when his salary depends upon his not understanding it."

(Sister) Elizabeth Kenny, *Australian nurse (developer of polio therapy), born Sep 20, 1886*
"Some minds remain open long enough for the truth not only to enter but to pass on through by way of a ready exit without pausing anywhere along the route."

Sophia Loren, *Italian actress, born Sofia Scicolone, Sep 20, 1934*
"Everything you see I owe to spaghetti."

SEPTEMBER 21

Restaurateurs' Day/Don't Cook Day
"Before marriage the three little words are 'I love you'; after marriage they are 'Let's eat out.' "—*Anon.*

"Wives who cook and do the dishes
Should be granted these three wishes:
A grateful mate,
A well-kissed cheek,
A restaurant dinner every week."—*Anon.*

"If I had my life to live over, I'd live over a delicatessen."—*Anon.*

"If God wanted me to cook and clean, my hands would be made of stainless steel."—*Anon.*

"I personally prefer a nice frozen TV Dinner at home, mainly because it's so little trouble. All you have to do is have another drink while you're throwing it in the garbage."—*Jack Douglas, American teacher and writer, born 1908 (birth date not available)*

"Manhattan is a narrow island off the coast of New Jersey devoted to the pursuit of lunch."—*Raymond Sokolov, American novelist and journalist, born 1941 (birth date not available)*

"I made my favorite thing for dinner: a reservation."—*Anon.*

SEPTEMBER 22

Postal Workers' Day
Office of United States Postmaster General established by Congress Sep 22, 1789.

Postal Workers' Day

"Old mailmen never quit; they just lose their zip."—*Anon.*

"Bad news travels fast ... unless it's in the mail."—*Anon.*

On mail damaged in handling by the Post Office: "With our automated equipment, it's amazing if a piece of mail even arrives."
    —*Postal Service employee*

Philip Dormer Stanhope, *English statesman and writer, born Sep 22, 1694*
    "Advice is seldom welcome; and those who want it the most always like it the least."

"Tommy" (Tom Charles) Lasorda, *American baseball player and manager, born Sep 22, 1927*
    "Never argue with people who buy ink by the gallon."

SEPTEMBER 23

Walter Lippmann, *American journalist, editor and writer, born Sep 23, 1889*

"Many a time I have wanted to stop talking and find out what I really believed."

Mickey Rooney, *American actor, born Joe Yule, Jr., Sep 23, 1920*
"You never know how happy you can be until you're married. And then it's too late."

"I'm the only man who has a marriage license made out 'To Whom It May Concern.'"

SEPTEMBER 24

Horace Walpole, *English novelist and letter writer, born Horatio Walpole, Sep 24, 1717*
At age 47, after his first big success: "It is charming to totter into vogue."

F(rancis) Scott Fitzgerald, *American novelist and short-story writer, born Sep 24, 1896*
"This being in love is great—you get a lot of compliments and begin to think you are a great guy."

"The cleverly expressed opposite of any generally accepted idea is worth a fortune to somebody."

"My stories written when sober are stupid."

Donald (Wickware) Brown, *American architect and artist, born Sep 24, 1927*
"There isn't enough coffee in the United States to keep everyone awake during a Presidential election campaign."

SEPTEMBER 25

Newspaper Day
First (and only) edition of the first American newspaper, "Publick Occurrences Both Foreign and Domestick," published Sep 25, 1690.

"The old saw says, 'Let a sleeping dog lie.' Right! Still, when there is much at stake it is better to get a newspaper to do it."—*Mark Twain*

William Faulkner, *American novelist, born Sep 25, 1897*
"There's no such thing as bad whiskey ... a man shouldn't fool with booze until he's fifty; then he's a damn fool if he doesn't."

Hollywood: "... the only place in the world where a man can get stabbed in the back while climbing a ladder."

"Red" (Walter Wellesley) Smith, *American sports columnist, born Sep 25, 1905*
"There's nothing to writing. All you do is sit down at a typewriter and open a vein."

SEPTEMBER 26

T(homas) S(tearns) Eliot, *English poet, critic and playwright, born Sep 26, 1888*

> "The difference between being an elder statesman
> And posing successfully as an elder statesman
> Is practically negligible."

"Immature poets imitate; mature poets steal."

"The years between 50 and 70 are the hardest. You are always being asked to do things and yet are not decrepit enough to turn them down."

> "How unpleasant to meet Mr. Eliot
> With his features of clerical cut
> And his brow so grim
> And his mouth so prim
> And his conversation so nicely
> Restricted to What Precisely
> And If and Perhaps and But."

Robert (Staughten) Lynd, *American teacher, editor and sociologist, born Sep 26, 1892*

"Friendship will not stand the strain of very much good advice for very long."

"It may well be that all games are silly. But then—so are human beings."

George Raft, *American actor, born George Ranft, Sep 26, 1895*

"Part of the loot went for gambling, part for horses, and part for women. The rest I spent foolishly." (He earned and spent about ten million dollars.)

SEPTEMBER 27

Ancestor Appreciation Day

"A man who prides himself on his ancestry is like the potato plant: the best part is underground."—*Spanish proverb*

> "Some people's money is merited
> And other people's is inherited."—*Ogden Nash*

SEPTEMBER 28

Georges Clemenceau, *French journalist, statesman and Premier, born Sep 28, 1841*

"America is the only nation in history which miraculously has gone directly from barbarism to degeneration without the usual interval of civilization."

"War is too important to be left to the generals."

Al Capp, *American cartoonist, born Alfred Gerald Caplin, Sep 28, 1909*
"Abstract art: a product of the untalented, sold by the unprincipled to the utterly bewildered."

Brigitte Bardot, *French actress, born Camille Javal, Sep 28, 1934*
"I'm not a myth people make me out to be. I'm a girl from a good respectable family who was very well *reared*."

"I started out as a lousy actress and have remained one."

"I've been condemned from more pulpits than Satan."

"Dan" (Daniel A.) Greenberg, *American teacher, editor and writer, born Sep 28, 1934*
"Storing your car in New York is safer than entering it in a demolition derby. But not much."

SEPTEMBER 29

Elizabeth Gaskell, *English novelist and biographer, born Elizabeth Cleghorn Stevenson, Sep 29, 1810*
"I'll not listen to reason.... Reason always means what someone else has to say."

Richard (Long) Harkness, *American journalist and broadcaster, born Sep 29, 1907*
"A committee is a group of the unwilling, picked from the unfit, to do the unnecessary."

SEPTEMBER 30

Truman Capote, *American novelist, short-story writer and playwright, born Truman Streckfus Persons, Sep 30, 1924*
"In California you lose a point off your IQ every year."

"In California everyone goes to a therapist, is a therapist, or is a therapist going to a therapist."

October

National Seafood Month

National Apple Month
National Car Care Month
National Sarcastics Month
National Cosmetology Month
 "A girl whose cheeks are covered with paint
 Has an advantage with me over one whose ain't."—*Ogden Nash*

National Pasta Month
> In 1966 the British Broadcasting Company showed a five-minute "documentary" on the growing of spaghetti in Italy, complete with film footage and reports about the dangers of the "spaghetti weevil."

National Pizza Month
> "The perfect lover is one who turns into a pizza at 4:00 AM."
> —*Charles Pierce (biographical information not available)*

National Seafood Month
> "My husband's on the seafood diet: whatever he sees, he eats."—*Anon.*

"FLOATING" HOLIDAYS THIS MONTH

Fire Prevention Week observed in United States week, Sunday thru Saturday, beginning second Sunday
> "Three failures and a fire make a Scotsman's fortune."
> —*Scottish saying*

At the grand opening of new custom-built headquarters for a Fire Brigade in Yorkshire, England, the enthusiasm of the celebration was dampened slightly after arrival of the building inspectors, who discovered a small error in the building—no fire escape.

National Bookkeepers' Week The Monday thru Friday that ends with the second Friday.

National Bookkeepers' Day: Friday of National Bookkeepers Week
> "The reason most bookkeepers wear glasses is that they've spent too much time watching their figures."—*Anon.*

"Old bookkeepers never quit; they just lose their balance."—*Anon.*

Child Health Day in United States

United Nations Universal Children's Day, the first Monday
> "Children are a great help. They are a comfort in your old age. And they help you reach it faster, too."—*Anon.*

"Life does not begin at the moment of conception or the moment of birth. It begins when the kids leave home and the dog runs away."—*Anon.*

"Children are unpredictable. You never know what inconsistency they're going to catch you in next."—*Franklin P. Jones, American attorney, born 1906 (birth date not available)*

"It's an epidemic: Parents are suffering from a sexually transmitted disease—children."—*Anon.*

"Children are natural mimics—they act like their parents in spite of every attempt to teach them good manners."—*Anon.*

> "Children aren't happy with nothing to ignore
> And that's what parents were created for."—*Ogden Nash*

Young children, according to a study, prefer adults who talk faster than normal. (So they can ignore more?)

Columbus Day observed in United States on the second Monday. Commemorates arrival of Columbus in the New World Oct 12, 1492

"October 12, the Discovery. It was wonderful to find America, but it would have been more wonderful to miss it."—*Mark Twain*

Thanksgiving Day in Canada second Monday

International Credit Union Day third Thursday

Mother-in-Law Day fourth Sunday

"A mother-in-law is the bark from the family tree."—*Anon.*

"Bigamy is a crime for which the extreme penalty is two mothers-in-law."—*Anon.*

"I know a mother-in-law who sleeps with her glasses on, the better to see her son-in-law suffer in her dreams."—*Ernest(-Alexander-Honoré) Coquelin, French actor, born 1848 (birth date not available)*

"My mother-in-law has come round to our house at Christmas seven years running. This year we're having a change. We're going to let her in."—*Les Dawson, English writer (birth date not available)*

Daylight Saving Time ends in United States last Sunday at 2 AM Fall back one hour.

"What we want is standard time for getting up and daylight saving time for quitting work."—*Anon.*

OCTOBER 1

World Vegetarian Day
"My favorite dish is mixed greens: twenties, fifties, and hundreds."—*Eileen Mason*

Happy Fiscal New Year, United States
"Isn't it a shame that future generations can't be here to see all the wonderful things we're doing with their money?"—*Anon.*

Austin O'Malley, *American oculist and writer, born Oct 1, 1858*
"An Englishman thinks seated; a Frenchman, standing; an American, pacing; an Irishman, afterward."

"A politician is like quicksilver. If you try to put your finger on him you will find nothing under it."

Louis Untermeyer, *American jeweler, poet, editor, anthologist, writer and critic, born Oct 1, 1885*
On his 90th birthday: "I'm writing my third autobiography ... the other two were premature."

"Jimmy" (James Earl) Carter (Jr.), *American farmer, politician, writer and 39th US President, born Oct 1, 1924*

"I don't know what people have got against Jimmy Carter. He's done nothing."—*Bob Hope about Jimmy Carter*

"I present an engineer's solution. Lay out the problem, lay out the possible solutions and then present a proposed answer. The trouble is that by the time I get to the answer, most people have quit listening."

Laurence Harvey, *English actor, born Larushka Mischa Skikne, Oct 1, 1928*

"Some of my best moments are spent with me."

Julie Andrews, *English actress and singer, born Julia Wells, Oct 1, 1935*

"Julie Andrews is like a nun with a switchblade."—*Leslie Halliwell about Julie Andrews*

"How does it feel to be a star? I suck my thumb a lot."

OCTOBER 2

"Mahatma" (Mohandas Karamchand) Gandhi, *Indian political and spiritual leader, born Oct 2, 1869*

Asked what he thought of Western civilization: "I think it would be a good idea."

"Groucho" (Julius Henry) Marx, *American actor and comedian, born Oct 2, 1890*

"A man is only as old as the woman he feels."

"Whoever named it 'necking' was a poor judge of anatomy."

"I never forget a face, but in your case I'll be glad to make an exception."

"Anyone who says he can see through women is missing a lot."

"I don't have a photograph, but you can have my footprints. They're upstairs in my socks."

Rex (Taylor) Reed, *American actor, columnist and critic, born Oct 2, 1938*

"Rex Reed is either at your feet or at your throat."—*Ava Gardner about Rex Reed*

"Beverly Hills ... is the only place in the world where the police have an unlisted telephone number."

OCTOBER 3

Thomas (Clayton) Wolfe, *American novelist, born Oct 3, 1900*

"I can always find plenty of women to sleep with, but the kind of woman that is really hard for me to find is a typist who can read my writing."

Gore Vidal, *American novelist, playwright, essayist, columnist and drama critic, born Oct 3, 1925*

"A good deed never goes unpunished."

"Litigation takes the place of sex at middle age."

"Teaching has ruined more American novelists than drink."

"Television is now so desperately hungry for material that they're scraping the top of the barrel."

"I'm all for bringing back the birch, but only between consenting adults."

"There is no human problem which could not be solved if people would simply do as I advise."

OCTOBER 4

(Alfred) Damon Runyon, *American journalist and short-story writer, born Oct 4, 1884*

"... always try to rub up against money, for if you rub up against money long enough, some of it may rub off on you."

"The race may not be to the swift nor the victory to the strong, but that's how you bet."

Alvin Toffler, *American journalist, teacher and writer, born Oct 4, 1928*

"Parenthood remains the greatest single preserve of the amateur."

OCTOBER 5

Expand Your Horizons Day

Robert Hutchings Goddard, *American teacher and physicist ("father of Space Age"), born Oct 5, 1882*

"If you aim for the moon and miss, you'll end up in the stars; if you aim for the barn door and miss, what you'll end up in isn't stardust."—*Anon.*

OCTOBER 6

Librarians' Day

American Library Association founded (Philadelphia, Pennsylvania) Oct 6, 1876

"We welcome sleepers here. A sleeping reader is less of a menace to the books than a waking one."—*Librarian at Cambridge University*

Carole Lombard, *American actress, born Jane Alice Peters, Oct 6, 1908*

"Hollywood is where they write the alibis before they write the story."

Ellen Frankfort, *American teacher, journalist and writer, born Oct 6, 1936*
"Choice has always been a privilege of those who could afford to pay for it."

OCTOBER 7

Niels (Henrik David) Bohr, *Danish physicist, born Oct 7, 1885*
"An expert is a man who has made all the mistakes which can be made, in a narrow field."

"Prediction is very difficult, especially about the future."

R(onald) D(avid) Laing, *Scottish psychiatrist and writer, born Oct 7, 1927*
"Few books today are forgivable."

(Bishop) Desmond (Mpilo) Tutu, *South African teacher, clergyman and political activist, born Oct 7, 1931*
"When the missionaries came to Africa they had the Bible and we had the land. They said 'Let us pray.' We closed our eyes. When we opened them we had the Bible and they had the land."

OCTOBER 8

"Bill" (William Edward) Vaughan, *American journalist and editor, born Oct 8, 1915*
"One trouble with growing older is that it gets progressively tougher to find a famous historical figure who didn't amount to much when he was your age."

"The Vice-Presidency is sort of like the last cookie on the plate. Everybody insists he won't take it, but somebody always does."

OCTOBER 9

Entrepreneurs' Day
"An entrepreneur is a self-employed person working 18 hours a day to avoid working 8 hours for someone else."—*Anon.*

"Any new venture goes through the following stages: enthusiasm, complication, disillusionment, search for the guilty, punishment of the innocent, and decoration of those who did nothing."—*Anon.*

"Experience is what you get when you expected something else." —*Anon.*

"When you can't find anyone to blame but yourself, it's time to hire help."—*Eileen Mason*

John Lennon, *English composer, musician and singer, born Oct 9, 1940*
"Life is what happens while you are making other plans."

OCTOBER 10

Committee/Conference Day
"A committee is a cul-de-sac down which ideas are lured and then quietly strangled."—*(Sir Thomas George) Barnett Cocks, English civil servant, born 1907 (birth date not available)*

"Conference: A place where conversation is substituted for the dreariness of labor and the loneliness of thought."—*Anon.*

Lin Yutang, *Chinese philologist, educator, editor and writer, born Oct 10, 1895*
"In order to appreciate the English language one has to have a certain contempt for logic."

OCTOBER 11

Gamblers' Day
"Nobody has ever bet enough on the winning horse."—*Anon.*

"I love poker because it's the only time you can beat a woman and not get put in jail."—*Thomas ("Amarillo Slim") Preston (biographical information not available)*

"It used to be if you wanted a horse to stand still, you tied it to a hitching post. Today, you just bet on it."—*Anon.*

OCTOBER 12

Garbage Collectors' Day
Overweight Chicago garbage collector Ruffs Jackson was ordered to lose 200 pounds or be fired. After reaching his goal through a crash diet, he was too weak to lift the garbage bins and was fired for inefficiency.

Jane (Sherwood) Ace, *American radio comedienne, born Oct 12, 1905*
"Time wounds all heels."

OCTOBER 13

(James) Stuart Keate, *Canadian journalist and newspaper publisher, born Oct 13, 1913*
"In any world menu, Canada must be considered the vichyssoise of nations—it's cold, half-French, and difficult to stir."

Garbage Collectors' Day

Lenny Bruce, *American comedian and screenwriter, born Leonard Alfred Schneider, Oct 13, 1925*

"Miami Beach is where neon goes to die."

Margaret (Hilda Roberts) Thatcher, *English politician and Prime Minister, born Oct 13, 1925*

"She has been beastly to the Bank of England, has demanded that the BBC 'set its house in order,' and tends to believe the worst of the Foreign and Commonwealth Office. She cannot see an institution without hitting it with her handbag."—*Julian Critchley about Margaret Thatcher*

"Mrs. Thatcher is doing for monetarism what the Boston Strangler did for door-to-door salesmen."—*Denis Healy about Margaret Thatcher*

"You and I come by road or rail, but economists travel on infrastructure."

"I am extraordinarily patient, provided I get my own way in the end."

"I'd like to go on being 35 for a long time."

OCTOBER 14

William Penn, *English Quaker leader and founder of Pennsylvania in US, born Oct 14, 1644*
"Men are generally more careful of the breed of their horses and dogs than of their children."

Katherine Mansfield, *New Zealand short-story writer, born Kathleen Beauchamp, Oct 14, 1888*
"To be wildly enthusiastic, or deadly serious—both are wrong.... One must keep ever present a sense of humor."

"I must say I hate money but it's the lack of it I hate most."

Dwight D(avid) Eisenhower, *American army officer and 34th US President, born Oct 14, 1890*
"Things have never been more like the way they are today in history."

"There is one thing about being President—nobody can tell you when to sit down."

e(dward) e(stlin) cummings, *American poet, playwright and artist, born Oct 14, 1894*
"I'm living so far beyond my income that we may almost be said to be living apart."

John (Robert) Wooden, *American basketball player and coach, born Oct 14, 1910*
"It's what you learn after you know it all that counts."

Roger (George) Moore, *English actor, born Oct 14, 1927*
"I replace everyone. I'll be replacing Mickey Mouse in about three years' time."

OCTOBER 15

National Grouch Day/World Poetry Day

"There once was a grouch named Jerry
Whose temper made everyone wary.
Though occasionally droll,
'Twas a fortunate soul
Who saw him smile last January."—*Anon.*

"Some mornings I wake up grouchy. Other days I let him sleep."
—*Anon.*

Friedrich Wilhelm Nietzsche, *German philosopher and poet, born Oct 15, 1844*
"One should never know too precisely whom one has married."

"When a man has been highly honored and has eaten a little he is most benevolent."

"For art to exist, for any sort of aesthetic activity or perception to exist, a certain physiological precondition is indispensable: intoxication."

"We praise or blame according to whether the one or the other offers a greater opportunity for our power of judgment to shine out."

"Woman was God's second mistake."

(Bishop) Charles (Henry) Colton, *American clergyman and writer, born Oct 15, 1848*
"Marriage is a feast where the grace is sometimes better than the dinner."

(Sir) P(elham) G(renville) Wodehouse, *English novelist, short-story writer and playwright, born Oct 15, 1881*
"To my daughter Leonora without whose never-failing sympathy and encouragement this book would have been finished in half the time."

George Sava, *English consulting surgeon and writer, born George Alexis Milkomanovich Milkomane, Oct 15, 1903*
"I make unpunctuality an art. The only time I am conscious of the time is when I am on time. Then I am frankly astonished."

John Kenneth Galbraith, *American economist, diplomat and writer, born Oct 15, 1908*
"Politics is not the art of the possible. It consists in choosing between the disastrous and the unpalatable."

"Economists are economical, among other things, of ideas. They make those they acquire as graduate students do for a lifetime."

"Lee" (Lido Anthony) Iacocca, *American engineer and automobile executive, born Oct 15, 1924*
"People want economy and they will pay any price to get it."

OCTOBER 16

Dictionary Day
Noah Webster, *American teacher, journalist and lexicographer, born Oct 16, 1758*
"The dictionary is nothing but a lot of words."—*Samuel Goldwyn*

National Boss Day
"Nothing is impossible ... if you don't have to do it yourself."—*Anon.*

"Before you have an argument with the boss, take a good look at both sides—her side and the outside."—*Anon.*

"Never put off until tomorrow what you can get someone else to do."—*Anon.*

"To err is human; to forgive is not company policy."—*Anon.*

"An executive is a person who has mastered the art of shuffling Credit and Blame back and forth between his In-Basket and his Out-Basket."—*Anon.*

"Executive ability is deciding quickly and getting somebody else to do the work."—*J.G. Pollard (biographical information not available)*

Oscar (Fingal O'Flahertie Wills) Wilde, *Irish poet, playwright and novelist, born Oct 16, 1854*

"Bachelors should be heavily taxed. It is not fair that some men should be happier than others."

"The London season is entirely matrimonial; people are either hunting for husbands or hiding from them."

"Children begin by loving their parents; as they grow older they judge them; sometimes they forgive them."

America is a country where "the young are always ready to give to those who are older than themselves the full benefits of their inexperience."

"If we men married the women we deserved, we should have a very bad time of it."

"There is only one thing in the world worse than being talked about, and that is not being talked about."

"The only way to get rid of temptation is to yield to it."

"After a good dinner, one can forgive anybody, even one's own relatives."

"Experience is the name everyone gives to their mistakes."

"The advantage of the emotions is that they lead us astray."

"The only thing to do with good advice is pass it on. It is never of any use to oneself."

"One should never make one's debut with a scandal. One should reserve that to give an interest to one's old age."

"In America I had two secretaries—one for autographs and the other for locks of hair. Within six months one had died of writer's cramp, and the other was completely bald."

"It is better to have a permanent income than be fascinating."

"There is much to be said in favour of modern journalism. By giving us the opinions of the uneducated, it keeps us in touch with the ignorance of the community."

"I feel that football is all very well as a game for rough girls but it is hardly suitable for delicate boys."

"Woman begins by resisting a man's advances and ends by blocking his retreat."

"Newspapers have degenerated. They may now be absolutely relied upon."

"My own business always bores me to death; I prefer other people's."

Arriving in New York Jan 3, 1882, he responded to customs officials who asked if he had anything to declare, "Nothing but my genius."

(Sir Joseph) Austen Chamberlain, *English statesman and writer, born Oct 16, 1863*
"He is more loyal to his friends than to his convictions."—*Margot Asquith about Austen Chamberlain*

Will Stanton, *American writer, born Oct 16, 1918*
"Getting a dog is like getting married. It teaches you to be less self-centered, to accept sudden, surprising outbursts of affection, and not to be upset by a few scratches on your car."

"Republicans study the financial pages of the newspaper. Democrats put them in the bottom of a bird cage."

OCTOBER 17

Do Something Daring Day
Evel Knievel, *American stunt performer, born Robert Craig, Oct 17, 1938*

Barnaby C(onrad) Keeney, *American historian and educator, born Oct 17, 1914*
"The scramble to get into college is going to be so terrible in the next few years that students are going to put up with almost anything, even an education."

OCTOBER 18

Logan Pearsall Smith, *American essayist and critic, born Oct 18, 1865*
"What is more enchanting than the voices of young people when you can't hear what they say?"

"A best seller is the gilded tomb of a mediocre talent."

A(bbott) J(oseph) Liebling, *American journalist and writer, born Oct 18, 1904*
"Freedom of the press belongs to those who own one."

George C(ampbell) Scott, *American actor and director, born Oct 18, 1927*
"He had a winning smile, but everything else was a loser."

On acting: "Don't you think it's a pretty spooky way to earn a living?"

OCTOBER 19

Keep Your Money Safe Day

The United States stock market crashed 510 points Oct 19, 1987.

"The jackasses outnumbered the bulls and the bears."—*Anon.*

"October. This is one of the peculiarly dangerous months to speculate in stocks. The others are July, January, September, April, November, May, March, June, December, August and February." —*Mark Twain*

"The best way to make a small fortune is to start with a big one." —*Anon.*

Lewis Mumford, *American historian, city planner, sociologist, teacher and writer, born Oct 19, 1895*

"Our national flower is the concrete cloverleaf."

"Layer upon layer, past times preserve themselves in the city until life itself is finally threatened with suffocation; then, in sheer defense, modern man invents the museum."

OCTOBER 20

Skydiving Day

First life saved by a parachute—Lieutenant (later Major General) Harold Harris Oct 20, 1922.

"The greatest thrill known to man isn't flying—it's landing." —*Anon.*

Adolph Deutsch, *American composer and conductor, born Oct 20, 1897*

"A film musician is like a mortician—he can't bring the body back to life, but he is expected to make it look better."

OCTOBER 21

Technology Day/Infomaniacs' Day

"If you're not scared to death, you haven't collected enough information."—*Eileen Mason*

"Technology is dominated by two types of people: those who understand what they do not manage, and those who manage what they do not understand."—*Anon.*

"Computers come in two varieties: the prototype and the obsolete."—*Anon.*

"Computer wizards never quit—they just lose their bytes."—*Anon.*

"The computer is a great invention. There are just as many mistakes as ever. But they are nobody's fault."—*Anon.*

Skydiving Day

"Some men are like musical glasses; to produce their finest tones, you must keep them wet."—*Samuel Taylor Coleridge, English poet, critic and philosopher, born Oct 21, 1772*

OCTOBER 22

Join a Club Day

"Please accept my resignation. I don't want to belong to any club that would accept me as a member."—*Groucho Marx*

A promotional piece for a private club's gala event installing its new president read: "The evening will conclude with a toast to the incoming president in champagne kindly supplied by the outgoing president, drunk as usual at midnight."

Timothy (Francis) Leary, *American psychologist, educator and drug cult leader, born Oct 22, 1920*
"Women who seek to be equal with men lack ambition."

OCTOBER 23

TV Talk Show Host Day

Frank (Lazarro) Rizzo, *American politician, born Oct 23, 1920*
As Philadelphia mayor: "The streets are safe in Philadelphia; it's only the people who make them unsafe."

Johnny Carson, *American television host and comedian, born Oct 23, 1925*
"I know a man who gave up smoking, drinking, sex, and rich food. He was healthy right up to the time he killed himself."

"Mail your packages early, so the post office can lose them in time for Christmas."

"I was so naive as a kid I used to sneak behind the barn and do nothing."

OCTOBER 24

International Forgiveness Day
"Forgive, O Lord, my little jokes on Thee
And I'll forgive Thy great big one on me."—*Robert Frost*

United Nations Day
United Nations founded Oct 24, 1945

"United Nations: Where America feeds the hands that bite it."
—*Gregory Nunn (biographical information not available)*

"United Nations: too many foreign countries living beyond our means."—*Anonymous American*

OCTOBER 25

National Magic Week Oct 25-31
"Magician: A person who lives within his income."—*Anon.*

"An amateur wizard named Polk
Wanted free of his marital yoke.
After much incantation
Came the vaporization
But 'twas Polk who vanished in smoke."—*Bruce Dexter*

Thomas Babington Macaulay, *English historian, poet, essayist and statesman, born Oct 25, 1800*
"Nothing is so useless as a general maxim."

Pablo (Ruiz y) Picasso, *Spanish painter and sculptor, born Oct 25, 1881*
"Picasso had a whim of iron."—*John Richardson about Pablo Picasso*

"Computers are useless. They can only give you answers."

When asked "How can you remember which paintings are yours?" he responded, "If I like it, I say it's mine. If I don't I say it's a fake."

"I am only a public entertainer who has understood his time."

"I'd like to live like a poor man with lots of money."

Anne Tyler, *American novelist, born Oct 25, 1941*
"While armchair travelers dream of going places, traveling armchairs dream of staying put."

OCTOBER 26

Optimists' Day
"An optimist is a person who starts a crossword puzzle with a fountain pen."—*Anon.*

"An optimist is a person who believes in marriage; a pessimist is a married optimist."—*Anon.*

"An optimist is a fellow who believes what's going to be will be postponed."—*Kin Hubbard*

OCTOBER 27

Folly Day
Desiderius Erasmus, *Dutch scholar (author of In Praise of Folly), born Oct 27, 1467*

"Fools rush in where fools have been before."—*Anon.*

"A little folly now and then
Is cherished by the wisest men."—*Anon.*

"It is folly to sing twice to a deaf man."—*English proverb*

"Muraglia bianca, carta di matto." (Italian) A white wall is the fool's paper.

"Delphinum natara doces." (Latin) You are teaching a dolphin to swim.

"Futility: playing a harp before a buffalo."—*Burmese proverb*

"When folly is bliss 'tis ignorance to be otherwise."—*Anon.*

Emily (Price) Post, *American etiquette authority, columnist and writer, born Oct 27, 1872*
> "... woman accepted cooking as a chore but man has made of it a recreation."

Enid Bagnold, *English novelist and playwright, born Oct 27, 1889*
> "Marriage. The beginning and the end are wonderful. But the middle part is hell."

Jack Carson, *Canadian actor and comedian, born Oct 27, 1910*
> "A fan club is a group of people who tell an actor's he's not alone in the way he feels about himself."

Dylan (Marlais) Thomas, *Welsh poet and playwright, born Oct 27, 1914*
> "I'm not at all sure that I want such a thing, myself, as a poetic film. I think films fine as they are, if only they were better!"

> On Wales: "The land of my fathers. And my fathers can have it."

> "Somebody's boring me.... I think it's me."

Willis Player, *American journalist and airline executive, born Oct 27, 1915*
> "A liberal is a person whose interests aren't at stake at the moment."

"Fran" (Frances Ann) Lebowitz, *American journalist and writer, born Oct 27, 1950*
> "She is the woman of Woody Allen's nightmares."—*Herbert Gold about Fran Lebowitz*

> "I never said I didn't like kids; adults I don't like. Kids don't review books."

> "If you are going to America, bring food."

> "Having been unpopular in high school is not just cause for book publication."

> "Ask your child what he wants for dinner only if he's buying."

> "Life is something to do when you can't get to sleep."

> "Success didn't spoil me; I've always been insufferable."

> "I never took an hallucinogenic because I never wanted my consciousness expanded one unnecessary iota."

OCTOBER 28

Immigrants' Day
> Statue of Liberty dedicated Oct 28, 1886.

> "Give me your tired, your poor ... as soon as they fill out forms 2478A through Z in triplicate."—*Anon.*

> "My forefathers didn't come over on the 'Mayflower,' but they met the boat."—*Will Rogers*

OCTOBER 29

James Boswell, *Scottish biographer, diarist, lawyer and essayist, born Oct 29, 1740*
"I think no innocent species of wit or pleasantry should be suppressed; and that a good pun may be admitted among the smaller excellencies of lively conversation."

(Hyppolyte-)Jean Giraudoux, *French diplomat, novelist and playwright, born Oct 29, 1882*
"No poet ever interpreted nature as freely as a lawyer interprets truth."

"Only the mediocre are always at their best."

OCTOBER 30

(Ambroise-)Paul(-Toussaint-Jules) Valéry, *French poet, essayist and critic, born Oct 30, 1871*
"The advantage of the incomprehensible is that it never loses its freshness."

"Politics is the art of preventing people from taking part in affairs which properly concern them."

"The purpose of psychology is to give us a completely different idea of the things we know best."

Ezra (Loomis) Pound, *American poet, essayist, critic and translator, born Oct 30, 1885*
On being released in April 1958, after 13 years in hospital and being declared incurably insane: "How did it go in the madhouse? Rather badly. But what other place could one live in America?"

Jean Rostand, *French biologist, novelist and writer, born Oct 30, 1894*
"Sometimes an admirer spends more talent extolling a work than the author did in creating it."

Ruth Gordon, *American actress and screenwriter, born Ruth Gordon Jones, Oct 30, 1896*
"The best impromptu speeches are the ones written well in advance."

"A little money helps, but what *really* gets it right is to *never*— I repeat—*never* under any condition face the facts."

Neil H(osler) McElroy, *American manufacturing executive and US Secretary of Defense, born Oct 30, 1904*
"In the space age, man will be able to go around the world in two hours—one for flying and the other to get to the airport."

OCTOBER 31

Halloween

Bobbing for apples originated with the Druids, whose New Year's Eve was October 31. Those who succeeded were guaranteed a prosperous year.

John Keats, *English poet, born Oct 31, 1795*

"... I have left no immortal work behind me—nothing to make my friends proud of my memory—but I have loved the principle of beauty in all things, and if I had had time I would have made myself remembered."

Lee Grant, *American actress, born Lyova Rosenthal, Oct 31, 1929*

"One's art adjusts to economic necessity if your metabolism does."

November

Aviation History Month

Aviation History Month
International Creativity Month

"FLOATING" HOLIDAYS THIS MONTH

American Education Week the Sunday thru Saturday preceding the fourth Thursday

"School days can be the happiest days of your life—if your kids are old enough to attend."—*Anon.*

"Don't let school get in the way of your education."—*Anon.*

"A good education is important. It enables you to pick out the most important things to worry about."—*Anon.*

"All most young people want out of school is themselves."—*Anon.*

"You can always spot an educated man. His opinions are the same as yours."—*Anon.*

"The advantage of a classical education is that it enables you to despise the wealth which it prevents you from achieving."—*Russell Green, English writer, born 1893 (birth date not available)*

"If a little knowledge is dangerous, where is the man who has so much as to be out of danger?"—*Anon.*

"Three reasons for being a teacher: June, July, and August."
—*Anon.*

"The only reason I always try to meet and know the parents better is because it helps me to forgive their children."—*Louis Johannot, Swiss schoolmaster (birth date not available)*

National Family Week observed in United States the Sunday thru Saturday including Thanksgiving

"God gives us relatives; thank God we can choose our friends."
—*Ethel W(atts) Mumford, American playwright, poet and novelist, born 1878 (birth date not available)*

"One would be in less danger
From the wiles of the stranger
If one's own kin and kith
Were more fun to be with."—*Ogden Nash*

General Election Day in United States the Tuesday after the first Monday (in election years)

"The only thing we learn from new elections is we learned nothing from the old."—*American proverb*

"Liberals have heart, conservatives have money, and the 'undecideds' have the deciding votes."—*Anon.*

"Get all the fools on your side and you can be elected to do anything."—*Frank Dane (biographical information not available)*

"We'd all like t' vote for th' best man, but he's never a candidate."
—*Kin Hubbard*

Sadie Hawkins Day first Saturday
(Women and girls ask men and boys out.)

Thanksgiving Day observed in United States the fourth Thursday
"On Thanksgiving Day, all over America, families sit down to
dinner at the same moment—halftime."—*Anon.*

"Thanksgiving is the time when the turkeys we elected a couple of
weeks before start telling us how they're going to tax the stuffing
out of us for the next four years."—*Bruce Dexter*

Shopping Weekend the Friday through Sunday after Thanksgiving
"Veni, vidi, Visa. (We came, we saw, we went shopping.)"
—*Jan Barrett (biographical information not available)*

"For that someone who has everything—send them the kids."
—*Anon.*

NOVEMBER 1

National Authors' Day
"Think much, speak little, and write less."—*French saying*

"The wages of sin are royalties."—*Jane Otten (biographical information not available)*

"Writers aren't exactly people.... They're a whole lot of people trying
to be one person."—*Anon.*

"Authors are easy enough to get on with—if you are fond of children."—*Michael Joseph, English journalist, consultant and writer,
born 1897 (birth date not available)*

"Originality is the art of concealing your sources."—*Anon.*

"The affair between Margot Asquith and Margot Asquith will live
as one of the prettiest love stories in all literature."—*Dorothy
Parker in a review of a book by Margot Asquith, English writer,
born Margaret Emma Alice Tennant, 1864 (birth date not available)*

"A story full of sparkling wit will keep its audience grinning,
Especially if the end of it is close to the beginning."—*Anon.*

"Strange that a man who has wit enough to write a satire should
have folly enough to publish it."—*Anon.*

Isaac Goldberg, *American writer and critic, born Nov 1, 1887*

"Diplomacy is to do and say
The nastiest thing in the nicest way."

NOVEMBER 2

Publishers' Day

"There is probably no hell for authors in the next world—they suffer too much from critics and publishers in this."—*Christian Nastell Boyce (biographical information not available)*

NOVEMBER 3

Sandwich Day

Sandwiches should be eaten with "a civilized swallow and not a barbarous bolt."—*John Montagu, Earl of Sandwich, English politician and diplomat, born Nov 3, 1718*

Montagu is said to have invented the sandwich as a time-saving snack to be eaten while he was engaged in 24-hour gambling sessions.

NOVEMBER 4

"Will" (William Penn Adair) Rogers, *American columnist, actor, writer and humorist, born Nov 4, 1879*

"A conference is just an admission that you want somebody to join you in your troubles."

"People that pay for things never complain. It's the guy you give something to that you can't please."

"The best thing about this group of candidates is that only one of them can win."

"Even when you make a tax form out on the level, you don't know when it's through if you are a crook or a martyr."

"An economist's guess is liable to be as good as anybody else's."

"The income tax has made liars out of more Americans than golf."

"The schools ain't what they used to be and never was."

"Politics ain't worrying this country one-tenth as much as where to find a parking place."

"More men have been elected between sundown and sunup than ever were elected between sunup and sundown."

"When you put down the good things you ought to have done, and leave out the bad ones you did do—that's Memoirs."

Robert (Milton) Bradbury (Jr.), *American architect, born Nov 4, 1924*

"A pedestrian is a man who has two cars—one being driven by his wife, the other by one of his children."

NOVEMBER 5

Ida (Minerva) Tarbell, *American journalist and writer, born Nov 5, 1857*
"There is no more effective medicine to apply to feverish public sentiment than figures."

Roy Rogers, *American actor, singer and restaurateur, born Leonard Franklin Slye, Nov 5, 1912*
"Times change. Nowadays it's a woman who's faster on the draw, and she can prove it at any bank window."

NOVEMBER 6

Boob Tube Day/Vidiot's Day
"Ninety-eight percent of American homes have TV sets... the people in the other two ... have to generate their own sex and violence."— *Franklin P. Jones, American attorney, born 1906 (birth date not available)*

"Television is really educational: Just think of all the repairmen's children it's putting through college."—*Anon.*

"I won't eat anything that has intelligent life, but I'd gladly eat a network executive or a politician."—*Marty Feldman, English comedian and actor, born 1933 (date of birth not available)*

"Professional wrestling's most mystifying hold is on its audience." —*Luke Neely (biographical information not available)*

The Japanese call the national passion for television "ichioku-so-hakuchi-ka," or "one hundred million people go crazy."

NOVEMBER 7

National Notary Public Day
(National Notary Public Week, the Sunday thru Saturday including Nov 7)

Leon Trotsky, *Russian journalist, revolutionary leader and writer, born Lev Davidovich Bronstein, Nov 7, 1879*
"If we had more time for discussion we should probably have made a great many more mistakes."

Albert Camus, *French novelist, playwright, essayist, journalist and philosopher, born Nov 7, 1913*
"Charm is a way of getting the answer 'yes' without asking a clear question."

"I conceived at least one great love in my life, of which I was always the object."

(Dame) Joan Sutherland, *Australian opera singer, born Nov 7, 1926*
"To be a diva, you've got to be absolutely like a horse."

NOVEMBER 8

Margaret Mitchell, *American novelist, born Nov 8, 1900*
"... the world can forgive practically anything except people who mind their own business."

Hollywood story editor Jacob Wilk was given an advance copy of a forthcoming novel by its enthusiastic publisher. He was so impressed that he urged his boss, Jack Warner, to buy a $50,000 option on the film rights. Warner refused, saying, "I wouldn't pay 50,000 bucks for any damn book any damn time." The book? *Gone with the Wind* by Margaret Mitchell, the best-selling novel in US history.

Katharine Hepburn, *American actress, born Nov 8, 1909*
"She ran the whole gamut of the emotions from A to B."—*Dorothy Parker about Katharine Hepburn*

"If you want to sacrifice the admiration of many men for the criticism of one, go ahead, get married."—*Advice of her mother to Katharine Hepburn*

"The average Hollywood film star's ambition is to be admired by an American, courted by an Italian, married to an Englishman and have a French boy friend."

NOVEMBER 9

Check the Batteries in Your Flashlight Day
Blackout of over 80,000 miles of East Coast of United States and Canada, Nov 9, 1965.

Marie Dressler, *Canadian actress, born Leila Marie Koerber, Nov 9, 1869*
"If ants are such busy workers, how come they find time to go to all the picnics?"

"I enjoy reading biographies because I want to know about the people who messed up the world."

Ed Wynn, *American actor, comedian, producer and songwriter, born Isaiah Leopold, Nov 9, 1886*
"Bachelor: A man who never makes the same mistake once."

Spiro (Theodore) Agnew, *American lawyer, politician and 39th US Vice President, born Nov 9, 1918*
"An intellectual is a man who doesn't know how to park a bike."

Check the Batteries in Your Flashlight Day

Joseph A(llen) Groff, *American soldier and civil servant, born Nov 9, 1925*
"My son is looking for an executive position so he can work his way down."

NOVEMBER 10

Martin Luther, *German priest, Biblical scholar, linguist and religious reformer, born Nov 10, 1483*

"Who loves not wine, woman and song
Remains a fool his whole life long."

Oliver Goldsmith, *Irish poet, novelist and playwright, born Nov 10, 1730*
"A book may be amusing with numerous errors, or it may be very dull without a single absurdity."

Martin (Henry) Fischer, *American physician, teacher and writer,*
born Nov 10, 1879
"A conclusion is the place where you got tired of thinking."

NOVEMBER 11

Veterans Day in United States

Remembrance Day in Canada and England

John (Ward) Leggett, *American novelist, born Nov 11, 1917*
"America, where overnight success is both a legend and a major
industry."

Robert Half, *American personnel agency executive, born Nov 11, 1918*
"A critic and a cricket are very much alike. They both make lots
of noise."

"No one is more ethical than someone who has just become ethical."

Kurt Vonnegut, Jr., *American novelist, born Nov 11, 1922*
"Educating a woman is like pouring honey over a fine Swiss watch.
It stops working."

NOVEMBER 12

Elizabeth Cady Stanton, *American leader of women's suffrage move-*
ment, born Nov 12, 1815
"Wherever the skilled hands and cultured brain of woman have
made the battle of life easier for man, he has readily pardoned her
sound judgment...."

"... one of the best gifts of the gods came to me in the form of a good,
faithful housekeeper."

NOVEMBER 13

Robert Louis (Balfour) Stevenson, *Scottish novelist, essayist, poet*
and critic, born Nov 13, 1850
"For God's sake give me the young man who has brains enough to
make a fool of himself."

NOVEMBER 14

Prince Charles (Philip Arthur George), *English royalty (son of*
Queen Elizabeth II), born Nov 14, 1948
"Falling madly in love with someone is not necessarily the starting
point to get married."

NOVEMBER 15

American Enterprise Day
"Under capitalism man exploits man; under socialism the reverse is true."—*Polish proverb*

"The flaw in the concept of 'free enterprise' is that only half of it is true."—*Bruce Dexter*

Franklin P(ierce) Adams, *American journalist, born Nov 15, 1881*
"There are plenty of good five-cent cigars in the country. The trouble is they cost a quarter. What this country really needs is a good five-cent nickel."

"The best part of the fiction in many novels is the notice that the characters are purely imaginary."

Aneurin Bevan, *English politician, born Nov 15, 1897*
"We know what happens to people who stay in the middle of the road. They get run over."

"I read the newspaper avidly. It is my one form of continous fiction."

Petula (Sally Olwen) Clark, *English singer and actress, born Nov 15, 1932*
"I thank God to be out of the country when my old movies come back on late-night television."

NOVEMBER 16

George S(imon) Kaufman, *American playwright and critic, born Nov 16, 1889*
"He's a real wolf: he can take one look at a girl and tell what kind of past she's going to have."

"I thought the play was frightful but I saw it under particularly unfortunate circumstances. The curtain was up."

NOVEMBER 17

Philatelic Societies Day
Society of Philaticians founded Nov 17, 1972.

Stamp collecting is the most popular hobby in the world—but maybe not for dieters: A United States postage stamp has about one-tenth of a calorie's worth of glue. (The hazards of licking and sticking.)

Shelby (Dade) Foote, *American novelist, playwright and historian, born Nov 17, 1916*
"Longevity conquers scandal every time."

NOVEMBER 18

(Sir) William S(chwenck) Gilbert, *English playwright, humorist and lyricist, born Nov 18, 1836*

> "Oh, don't the days seem lank and long,
> When all goes right and nothing goes wrong?
> And isn't your life extremely flat
> With nothing whatever to grumble at?"

"I know how good I am, but I do not know how bad I am."

Dorothy Dix, *American advice columnist, born Elizabeth Meriwether Gilmer, Nov 18, 1870*

"Drying a widow's tears is one of the most dangerous occupations known to man."

"Nobody wants to kiss when they are hungry."

"My husband keeps telling me to go to hell. Have I a legal right to take the children?"—*Letter to Dorothy Dix*

Charles Edwin Woodrow Bean, *Australian journalist and historian, born Nov 18, 1879*

"Australia is a big blank map, and the whole people is constantly sitting over it like a committee, trying to work out the best way to fill it in."

(Percy) Wyndham Lewis, *English painter, novelist and critic, born Nov 18, 1882*

"New York is, after all, a place of business; it is not constructed to be lived in."

NOVEMBER 19

George Rogers Clark, *American frontiersman and soldier, born Nov 19, 1752*

"The only thing that continues to give us more for our money is the weighing machine."

Peter (Ferdinand) Drucker, *American educator, business consultant and writer, born Nov 19, 1909*

"Whenever a man's failure can be traced to management's mistakes, he has to be kept on the payroll."

"Ted" (Robert Edward) Turner (III), *American sportsman and broadcasting executive, born Nov 19, 1938*

"Life is like a B-grade movie. You don't want to leave in the middle of it, but you don't want to see it again."

"If only I had a little humility I would be perfect."

NOVEMBER 20

Gene Tierney, *American actress, born Nov 20, 1920*
"I had no trouble playing any kind of role. My problems began when I had to be myself."

Robert F(rancis) Kennedy, *American lawyer, politician and US Attorney General, born Nov 20, 1925*
"One fifth of the people are against everything all the time."

NOVEMBER 21

World Hello Day
(Say hello to ten strangers.)

"A wise man knows everything; a shrewd one, everybody."—*Anon.*

Fallen Idols Day
Rebecca Felton became the first woman United States Senator Nov 21, 1922. She was appointed, to fill a vacancy, by the governor of

World Hello Day: Say hello to ten strangers.

Georgia, who said, "There are now no limitations upon the ambitions of women." There were on Ms. Felton, however: all that remained unexpired of the term was one day.

Voltaire, *French novelist, playwright, poet, historian, critic and philosopher, born François-Marie Arouet, Nov 21, 1694*

"Men will always be mad and those who think they can cure them are the maddest of all."

"I advise you to go on living solely to enrage those who are paying your annuities. It is the only pleasure I have left."

"The world is a vast temple dedicated to Discord."

"I was never ruined but twice—once when I lost a lawsuit, once when I won one."

"It is not enough to be exceptionally mad, licentious and fanatical in order to win a great reputation; it is still necessary to arrive on the scene at the right time."

"My prayer to God is a very short one: 'O Lord, make my enemies ridiculous.' God has granted it."

He once sent a passionate letter that began, "My Dear Hortense," but absent-mindedly closed, "Farewell, my dear Adele."

Hugh Kingsmill, *English biographer, critic, novelist and anthologist, born Hugh Kingsmill Lunn, Nov 21, 1889*

"Friends are God's apology for relations."

NOVEMBER 22

George Eliot, *English novelist, born Mary Ann Evans, Nov 22, 1819*

"The happiest women, like the happiest nations, have no history."

"A different taste in jokes is a great strain on the affections."

"I'm not denyin' the women are foolish: God Almighty made 'em to match the men."

Rodney Dangerfield, *American comedian and actor, born Jacob Cohen, Nov 22, 1921*

"After two days in the hospital I took a turn for the nurse."

"At my age, I want two girls at once; if I fall asleep, they have each other to talk to."

"If it weren't for pickpockets I'd have no sex life at all."

Billie Jean King, *American tennis player, born Nov 22, 1943*

"I change my mind so often that whatever the situation is, it's usually totally different by the time a particular item sees print."

NOVEMBER 23

Judge's Day

"A judge is a law student who marks his own examination papers."—*H.L. Mencken*

"Corn can't expect justice from a court composed of chickens."
—*African proverb*

"How to win a case in court: If the law is on your side, pound on the law; if the facts are on your side, pound on the facts; if neither is on your side, pound on the table."—*Anon.*

The first dark glasses were invented in China in the fifteenth century, not to ward off the sun's rays, but to conceal the expressions of judges in court.

"Willie the Lion" Smith, *American jazz pianist, born William Henry Joseph Berthol Bonaparte, Nov 23, 1897*

"Romance without finance is no good."

NOVEMBER 24

Laurence Sterne, *English novelist, born Nov 24, 1713*

"I live in a constant endeavour to fence against the infirmities of ill health, and other evils of life, by mirth; being firmly persuaded that every time a man smiles, but much more so, when he laughs, that it adds something to this Fragment of Life."

(Alan) Geoffrey Cotterell, *English novelist and short-story writer, born Nov 24, 1919*

"In America only the successful writer is important, in France all writers are important, in England no writer is important and in Australia you have to explain what a writer is."

John V(liet) Lindsay, *American lawyer, politician and writer, born Nov 24, 1921*

"The miniskirt enables young ladies to run faster, and because of it, they may have to."

William F(rank) Buckley, Jr., *American editor, columnist, television interviewer and writer, born Nov 24, 1925*

"... a fool who spends too much time caressing dictionaries."
—*Merle Kessler about William F. Buckley, Jr.*

NOVEMBER 25

Intemperance Day

Carry Nation, *American temperance leader, born Carry Amelia Moore, Nov 25, 1846*

"A lady temperance candidate concluded her passionate oration: 'I would rather commit adultery than take a glass of beer.' Whereupon a clear voice from the audience asked 'Who wouldn't?' "
—*Adlai Ewing Stevenson*

Toast: "Here's to abstinence. May we always practice it in moderation."—*Anon.*

Joseph Wood Krutch, *American teacher, essayist, critic and conservationist, born Nov 25, 1893*
"Logic is the art of going wrong with confidence."

Virgil Thomson, *American composer, conductor and music critic, born Nov 25, 1896*
"Every composer's music reflects ... the source of the money the composer is living on while writing the music."

NOVEMBER 26

William Cowper, *English poet, translator and editor, born Nov 26, 1731*

"How much a dunce that has been sent to roam
Excels a dunce that has been kept at home!"

(Arnold) Eric Sevareid, *American broadcast journalist, born Nov 26, 1912*
"The chief cause of problems is solutions."

Charles (Monroe) Schulz, *American cartoonist, born Nov 26, 1922*
"There's a difference between a philosophy and a bumper sticker."

"I know the answer! The answer lies within the heart of all mankind! The answer is twelve? I think I'm in the wrong building."

"I have a new philosophy. I'm only going to dread one day at a time."

NOVEMBER 27

James Agee, *American novelist, poet and film critic, born Nov 27, 1909*
"The English instinctively admire any man who has no talent and is modest about it."

NOVEMBER 28

Tinkerers Day (All it takes is imagination and a high tolerance for disorder.)

"He is very fond of making things which he doesn't want, and then giving them to people who have no use for them."—*Anon.*

William Blake, *English poet and artist, born Nov 28, 1757*
"Thy friendship oft has made my heart to ache:
Do be my enemy—for friendship's sake."

"Those who restrain Desire, do so because theirs is weak enough to be restrained."

Rita Mae Brown, *American poet, critic and writer, born Nov 28, 1944*
"Lead me not into temptation; I can find the way myself."

NOVEMBER 29

Louisa May Alcott, *American novelist, born Nov 29, 1832*
"People don't have fortunes left them ... nowadays; men have to work, and women to marry for money. It's a dreadfully unjust world...."

"... rivalry adds so much to the charms of one's conquests."

"House-keeping ain't no joke."

"My definition [of a philosopher] is of a man up in a balloon, with his family and friends holding the ropes which confine him to the earth and trying to haul him down."

"... elegance has a bad effect upon my constitution...."

"A little kingdom I possess,
Where thoughts and feelings dwell;
And very hard the task I find
Of governing it well."

George Gilder, *American economist and writer, born Nov 29, 1939*
"When I was single, I was preoccupied with sex. Now that I'm an elder statesman, I've moved on to a more dignified concern: preoccupation with money."

NOVEMBER 30

Mark Twain, *American journalist, river pilot, lecturer and humorous writer, born Samuel Langhorne Clemens, Nov 30, 1835*
"Most writers regard the truth as their most valuable possession, and therefore are most economical in its use."

"Familiarity breeds contempt—and children."

"What is the difference between a taxidermist and a tax collector: The taxidermist takes only your skin."

"To eat is human
To digest divine."

"Confession may be good for my soul, but it sure plays hell with my reputation."

"All you need in this life is ignorance and confidence, and then Success is sure."

"Every man has a secret ambition—to outsmart horses, fish and women."

"Part of the secret of success in life is to eat what you like and let the food fight it out inside."

"Few things are harder to put up with than a good example."

"It usually takes me more than three weeks to prepare a good impromptu speech."

"When I was younger I could remember anything, whether it had happened or not."

"Get your facts first, then you can distort them as you please."

"Reader, suppose you were an idiot; and suppose you were a member of Congress; but I repeat myself...."

"I was gratified to be able to answer promptly. I said 'I don't know.' "

"In the first place, God made idiots. That was for practice. Then he made school boards."

"There are few things that are so unpardonably neglected in our country as poker. The upper class knows very little about it. Now and then you find ambassadors who have a sort of general knowledge of the game, but the ignorance of the people is fearful. Why, I have known clergymen, good men, kindhearted, liberal, sincere, and all that, who did not know the meaning of a flush. It is enough to make one ashamed of one's species."

"It is by the grace of God that in our country we have those three unspeakably precious things: freedom of speech, freedom of conscience, and the prudence never to practise either of them."

"Sometimes too much to drink is barely enough."

"There are two times in a man's life when he should not speculate: when he can't afford it, and when he can."

"I'm opposed to millionaires, but it would be dangerous to offer me the position."

"I don't mind what the opposition says of me, so long as they don't tell the truth."

(Sir) Winston (Leonard Spencer) Churchill, *English statesman,*
writer and Prime Minister, born Nov 30, 1874

"Winston has devoted the best years of his life to preparing
his impromptu speeches."—*Frederick Edwin Smith about*
Winston Churchill

What a politician needs: "It is the ability to foretell what is going to
happen tomorrow, next week, next month, and next year. And to
have the ability afterwards to explain why it didn't happen."

"Politics are almost as exciting as war. In war you can only be killed
once, but in politics many times."

"The English never draw a line without blurring it."

"A fanatic is one who can't change his mind and won't change
the subject."

On Calcutta: "I shall always be glad to have seen it—
for the same reason Papa gave for being glad to have seen Lisbon—
namely, 'that it will be unnecessary ever to see it again.' "

"Headmasters have powers at their disposal with which Prime
Ministers have never yet been invested."

"An appeaser is one who feeds a crocodile hoping it will eat
him last."

"History will be kind to me for I intend to write it."

He was the first honorary citizen of the United States.

December

Party Training Month

Universal Human Rights Month

Party Training Month

During your holiday celebrations, try not to *suilk* [Scottish: swallow, gulp, or suck with a slobbering noise], and watch out for the *Katzenjammer* [German: monumentally severe hangover]. Let your *ondinnonk* [Iroquoian: the soul's innermost benevolent desires, the urge to do something good for somebody] be your guide, and your

204

gifts be free of *carità pelosa* [Italian: "hairy" generosity, or generosity with an ulterior motive]. And may you enjoy *tjotjog* [Javanese: harmonious congruence in human affairs].

"Our customers are party trained."—*Anonymous tavern owner*

"FLOATING" HOLIDAYS THIS MONTH

Annual announcement of "The Most Boring Celebrities of the Year" by The Boring Institute third Monday

Underdog Day third Friday
(Salute an unsung hero.)

"If fame comes after death, I'm in no hurry for it."—*Martial, Roman epigrammist and poet*

"If he did not succeed, he at least failed in a glorious undertaking."—*Ovid, Roman poet*

Winter Solstice in Northern Hemisphere (Winter Begins) about Dec 22

"If you don't believe hell freezes over, you haven't been to Nome [Alaska]."—*Lucky Severson (biographical information not available)*

DECEMBER 1

Sit Down for Your Rights Day
Mrs. Rosa Parks, a black seamstress from Montgomery, Alabama, was arrested for refusing to give her seat at the front of the bus to a white man on Dec 1, 1955.

"A man of courage never needs weapons, but he may need bail." —*Anon.*

Oliver (Brooke) Herford, *English poet, writer, illustrator and wit, born Dec 1, 1863*
"Manuscript: something submitted in haste and returned at leisure."

Woody Allen, *American actor, director, producer and writer, born Allen Stewart Konigsberg, Dec 1, 1935*
"Basically my wife was immature. I'd be at home in the bath and she'd come in and sink my boats."

"Money is better than poverty, if only for financial reasons."

"I had a tendency to place my wife under a pedestal."

"When I was kidnapped, my parents snapped into action. They rented out my room."

"Didn't you think it was strange he was married and yet he still couldn't get a date for New Year's Eve?"

"If my film makes one more person miserable, I'll feel I've done my job."

Richard Pryor, *American comedian and actor, born Dec 1, 1940*
"Marriage is really tough because you have to deal with feelings and lawyers."

Bette Midler, *American singer and actress, born Dec 1, 1945*
"After thirty, a body has a mind of its own."

"If sex is such a natural phenomenon, how come there are so many books on 'how to'?"

"I never know how much of what I say is true."

DECEMBER 2

Journalists' Day
"Good taste is, of course, an utterly dispensable part of any journalist's equipment."—*Michael Hogg, English teacher and writer, born 1954 (birth date not available)*

"A newspaper editorial writer is one who comes down from the observation post after the battle is over and shoots the wounded." —*Anon.*

(Joseph) Russell Lynes (Jr.), *American editor and writer, born Dec 2, 1910*
"Every journalist has a novel in him, which is an excellent place for it."

DECEMBER 3

Joseph Conrad, *English novelist and short-story writer, born Józef Teodor Konrad Korzeniowski, Dec 3, 1857*
"Gossip is what no one claims to like, but everybody enjoys."

"Great achievements are accomplished in a blessed, warm mental fog."

"Being a woman is a terribly difficult trade, since it consists principally of dealing with men."

DECEMBER 4

Thomas Carlyle, *Scottish essayist and historian, born Dec 4, 1795*
"It was good of God to let Carlyle and Mrs. Carlyle marry one

another and so make only two people miserable instead of four."
  —*Samuel Butler on the marriage in 1827 of Jane Welsh and Thomas Carlyle*

"There is a great discovery still to be made in literature, that of paying literary men by the quantity they do not write."

"If you are ever in doubt as to whether or not you should kiss a pretty girl, always give her the benefit of the doubt."

"A well-written life is almost as rare as a well-spent one."

Samuel Butler, *English satirist and novelist, born Dec 4, 1835*
  "Brigands demand your money or your life; women require both."

"Life is the art of drawing sufficient conclusions from insufficient premises."

"All progress is based upon a universal innate desire of every organism to live beyond its income."

"Men are seldom more commonplace than on supreme occasions."

"The world can ill spare any vice which has obtained long and large among civilized people."

"Man is the only animal that laughs and has a state legislature."

"God cannot alter the past, but historians can."

"It is the function of vice to keep virtue within reasonable bounds."

"I do not mind lying, but I hate inaccuracy."

Alan Gregg, *American novelist, short-story writer and editor, born Gertrude Ethel Mallette, Dec 4, 1887*
  "A good education should leave much to be desired."

DECEMBER 5

International Volunteer Day for Economic and Social Development
United Nations Volunteers program established Dec 5, 1970.

Don't Drink Water Day
  Prohibition repealed in United States Dec 5, 1933.
  During the 13 years that Prohibition was enforced by the Treasury Department, the Department of Agriculture continued to distribute leaflets telling how to extract alcohol from apples, bananas, pumpkins, and all manner of produce.

  "One drink is just right; two is too many; three are too few."—*Spanish saying*

  "I drink no more than a sponge."—*François Rabelais, French monk, physician and novelist, born c.1483 (birth date not available)*

  "Wine improves with age—the older I get, the more I like it."—*Anon.*

  "Reality is a delusion created by an alcohol deficiency."—*Anon.*

"One dares not eat on an empty stomach."—*Eileen Mason*

"Walt" (Walter Elias) Disney, *American producer and animation pioneer, born Dec 5, 1901*

> "I've always had a nightmare. I dream that one of my pictures has ended up in an art theater. And I wake up shaking."

> "I love Mickey Mouse more than any woman I've ever known."

Calvin (Marshall) Trillin, *American columnist and writer, born Dec 5, 1935*

> "It happens to be a matter of record that I was first in print with the discovery that the tastelessness of the food offered in American clubs varies in direct proportion to the exclusiveness of the club."

> "Marriage, as I have often remarked, is not merely sharing one's fettucine but sharing the burden of finding the fettucine restaurant in the first place."

DECEMBER 6

Charles John Darling, *English jurist, politician, poet and writer, born Dec 6, 1849*

> "To sacrifice one's honour to one's party is so unselfish an act that our most generous statesmen have not hesitated to do it."

(Sir Francis) Osbert (Sacheverell) Sitwell, *English poet, novelist, short-story writer and critic, born Dec 6, 1892*

> "I am most fond of talking and thinking; that is to say, talking first and thinking afterwards."

> "The men of the Golden Horde were almost as kind to children as to horses—though naturally they regarded them with less reverence."

Steven Wright, *American actor and comedian, born Dec 6, 1955*

> "I have an existential map. It has 'You are here' written all over it."

DECEMBER 7

(Matthew) Heywood (Campbell) Broun, *American journalist and novelist, born Dec 7, 1888*

> "Posterity is as likely to be wrong as anybody else."

> "The only real argument for marriage is that it remains the best method for getting acquainted."

"Bo" (Robert) Belinsky, *American baseball player, born Dec 7, 1936*

> "Bo was an appealing rogue and it is good to see the wastrels of the world win one now and then."—*Gene Autry about Bo Belinsky*

"I have an existential map. It has 'You are here'
written all over it."

Howard Finkelstein, *American lawyer, born Dec 7, 1951*
"Lawyers are experts at keeping people from reaching any kind
of agreement."

DECEMBER 8

Hervey Allen, *American poet, novelist and biographer, born William*
Harvey Allen, Jr., Dec 8, 1889
"Religions change; beer and wine remain."

James (Grover) Thurber, *American humorous artist and author,*
born Dec 8, 1894
"Well, if I called the wrong number, why did you answer the
phone?"

"A woman's place is in the wrong."

"You can fool too many of the people too much of the time."

"Some American writers who have known each other for years have never met in the daytime or when both were sober."

"There is something about a poet which leads us to believe that he died, in many cases, as long as 20 years before his birth."

"I hate women because they always know where things are."

Maximilian Schell, *Austrian actor and producer, born Dec 8, 1930*
"I always said I won't marry until I go to Japan and see the beautiful women there. I've been to Japan now, and I have to have another excuse."

DECEMBER 9

Hermione (Ferdinanda) Gingold, *English actress, critic and writer, born Dec 9, 1897*
"My father dealt in stocks and shares and my mother also had a lot of time on her hands."

"There are too many men in politics and not enough elsewhere."

"Fighting is essentially a masculine idea; a woman's weapon is her tongue."

"I got all the schooling an actress needs. That is, I learned to write enough to sign contracts."

John Cassavetes, *American screenwriter, actor, director and producer, born Dec 9, 1929*
"I never know what my movies are about until I finish them."

DECEMBER 10

Human Rights Day
United Nations adopted "Universal Declaration of Human Rights" Dec 10, 1948. (Human Rights Week Dec 10-16)

Nobel Prizes awarded
Alfred Nobel, Swedish chemist and engineer (inventor of dynamite), died on Dec 10, 1896. In his will he established the Nobel Prize.

Emily (Elizabeth) Dickinson, *American poet, born Dec 10, 1830*
"Tell the truth
But tell it slant."

"It is essential to the sanity of mankind that each one should think the other crazy...."

"If I feel physically as if the top of my head were taken off, I know that is poetry."

Only seven of her poems were published during her lifetime.

James H(arlan) Boren, *American teacher, writer and businessman,*
born Dec 10, 1925
"I got the bill for my surgery. Now I know what those doctors were
wearing masks for."

DECEMBER 11

Fiorello (Henry) La Guardia, *American lawyer and politician,*
born Dec 11, 1882
"We have had two chickens in every pot, two cars in every garage,
and now we have two headaches for every aspirin."

"When I make a mistake it's a beaut."

DECEMBER 12

Gustave Flaubert, *French novelist, born Dec 12, 1821*
"Of all the icy blasts that blow on love, a request for money is the
most chilling and havoc-wreaking."

Frederick (Adolphus) Sawyer, *American politician, born*
Dec 12, 1822
"A diplomat is a man who thinks twice before he says nothing."

"Frank" (Francis Albert) Sinatra, *American singer and actor,*
born Dec 12, 1915
On Hollywood reporters: "All day long, they lie in the sun, and
when the sun goes down, they lie some more."

"I'm for anything that gets you through the night, be it prayer,
tranquilizers or Jack Daniels."

"If I had as many love affairs as you fellows have given me credit
for, I would now be speaking to you from inside a jar at the Harvard
Medical School."

DECEMBER 13

(Christian Johann) Heinrich Heine, *German poet, journalist and*
critic, born Chaim Harry Heine, Dec 13, 1797
"Experience is a good school, but the fees are high."

"Silence: a conversation with an Englishman."

"The Romans would never have found time to conquer the world if
they had first been obliged to learn Latin."

He left his estate to his wife on the condition that she remarry, explaining in his will, "Then there will be at least one man to regret my death."

George (Pratt) Shultz, *American economist and US Secretary of State, born Dec 13, 1920*

"I learned in business that you had to be very careful when you told somebody that's working for you to do something, because the chances were very high he'd do it. In government, you don't have to worry about that."

DECEMBER 14

Halcyon Days Dec 14-28   a time of calm and tranquillity

The ancients believed a fabled bird called the "halcyon" calmed the wind and waves during this time.

Leon Botstein, *American educator, historian and musician, born Dec 14, 1946*

"At best, most college presidents are running something that is somewhere between a faltering corporation and a hotel."

DECEMBER 15

Bill of Rights Day   The first ten amendments to the United States Constitution, known as the Bill of Rights, became effective Dec 15, 1791.

"We still have the rights but the bill's getting higher."—*Bruce Dexter*

"A dictatorship is the kind of government where anything that's not obligatory is forbidden."—*Anon.*

Jean Paul Getty, *American oil man, born Dec 15, 1892*

"If you get up early, work late, and pay your taxes, you will get ahead—if you strike oil."

"The weak shall inherit the earth—but not the mineral rights."

Richard (Howard Stafford) Crossman, *English teacher, statesman and writer, born Dec 15, 1907*

"He is a man of opinions, most of them of short duration."—*Bessie Braddock about Richard Crossman*

Tim Conway, *American comedian and actor, born Dec 15, 1933*

"It wasn't actually a divorce. I was traded."

DECEMBER 16

Jane Austen, *English novelist, born Dec 16, 1775*
"I do not want people to be very agreeable, as it saves me the trouble of liking them a great deal."

"A lady's imagination is very rapid; it jumps from admiration to love, from love to matrimony, in a moment."

(George) Santayana, *American philosopher, poet and novelist, born Jorge Augustín Nicolás Ruiz de Santayana, Dec 16, 1863*
"It is part of prudence to thank an author for his book before reading it, so as to avoid the necessity of lying about it afterwards."

"Fanaticism consists in redoubling your effort when you have forgotten your aim."

"Those who cannot remember the past are condemned to repeat it."

"Never have I enjoyed youth so thoroughly as I have in my old age."

(Sir) Noël Coward, *English playwright, actor and composer, born Dec 16, 1899*
"People are wrong when they say the opera isn't what it used to be. It is what it used to be. That's what's wrong with it."

"I've over-educated myself in all the things I shouldn't have known at all."

"I write at high speed because boredom is bad for my health."

He first appeared on the London stage when he was ten.

Margaret Mead, *American anthropologist and writer, born Dec 16, 1901*
"Women want mediocre men, and men are working hard to be as mediocre as possible."

Frank Deford, *American radio/television commentator, novelist, editor and writer, born Dec 16, 1938*
"In Hollywood, writers are considered only the first drafts of human beings."

DECEMBER 17

Wright Brothers Day/Pan American Aviation Day
Orville and Wilbur Wright, American aviation pioneers, made first powered flight (near Kitty Hawk, North Carolina) on Dec 17, 1903.

"If God had really intended men to fly, he'd make it easier to get to the airport."—*George Winters (biographical information not available)*

"If airport traffic continues to snarl, the only sure way to get there on Tuesday will be to leave on Monday."—*David Pauly (biographical information not available)*

Wright Brothers Day/Pan American Aviation Day

"People who fly into a rage seldom make a smooth landing."—*Anon.*

Ludwig van Beethoven, *German musician and composer, baptized Dec 17, 1770 (birth date not available)*

The *Philadelphia Bulletin* (now extinct, and no wonder) once ran the following item: "Beethoven had ten children and practiced on a spinster in the attic."

Ford Maddox Ford, *English novelist, editor and critic, born Ford Hermann Hueffer, Dec 17, 1873*

"His mind was like a Roquefort cheese, so ripe that it was palpably falling to pieces."—*Van Wyck Brooks about Ford Maddox Ford*

William Safire, *American columnist and writer, born Dec 17, 1929*
"Is sloppiness in speech caused by ignorance or apathy? I don't know and I don't care."

DECEMBER 18

George D(enison) Prentice, *American journalist, poet and writer, born Dec 18, 1802*
> "There are two periods when Congress does no business: one is before the holidays, and the other after."

Saki, *English journalist, novelist and short-story writer, born Hector Hugh Munro, Dec 18, 1870*
> "A little inaccuracy sometimes saves tons of explanation."

> "You can't expect a boy to be vicious till he's been to a good school."

> "All decent people live beyond their income nowadays, and those who aren't respectable live beyond other people's. A few gifted individuals manage to do both."

> "Monogamy is the Western custom of one wife and hardly any mistresses."

> "The sacrifices of friendship were beautiful in her eyes so long as she was not asked to make them."

> "People may say what they like about the decay of Christianity; the religious system that produced green Chartreuse can never really die."

DECEMBER 19

(Sir) Ralph (David) Richardson, *English actor, born Dec 19, 1902*
> "The most precious things in speech are the pauses."

> "The art of acting consists of keeping people from coughing."

DECEMBER 20

Siblings' Day
> "Where there's a sibling
> There's quibbling."
> —*Selma Raskin (biographical information not available)*

> "There is only one good substitute for the endearments of a sister, and that is the endearments of some other fellow's sister."
> —*Josh Billings*

> "Nepotism is only kin deep."—*Anon.*

Hortense Calisher, *American novelist, born Dec 20, 1911*
> "A happy childhood can't be cured. Mine'll hang around my neck like a rainbow ... instead of a noose."

DECEMBER 21

Benjamin Disraeli, *English statesman, novelist and Prime Minister, born Dec 21, 1804*

> "When a man fell into his anecdotage it was a sign for him to retire from the world."

> "Next to knowing when to seize an opportunity, the most important thing in life is to know when to forgo an advantage."

(Dame) Rebecca West, *English journalist, novelist and critic, born Cicily Isabel Fairfield, Dec 21, 1892*

> "Most works of art, like most wines, ought to be consumed in the district of their fabrication."

> "It is queer how it is always one's virtues and not one's vices that precipitate one into disaster."

> "The point is that nobody likes having salt rubbed into their wounds, even if it is the salt of the earth."

Anthony (Dymoke) Powell, *English novelist, born Dec 21, 1905*

> "Self-love seems so often unrequited."

> "In this country it is rare for anyone, let alone a publisher, to take writers seriously."

Jane Fonda, *American actress, born Dec 21, 1937*

> "Before I went into analysis, I told everyone lies—but when you spend all that money, you tell the truth."

> On acting: "You spend your life doing something they put people in asylums for."

DECEMBER 22

Duffers' Day

United States Golf Association formed Dec 22, 1894.

> "Most of the people who do great things in life are alone— especially on a golf course."—*Anon.*

> "Old golfers never quit; they just putter around."—*Anon.*

> "Some golfers know more ways to slice than a food processor." —*Anon.*

> "Golf has given me an understanding of the futility of human effort."—*Ebra Eban (biographical information not available)*

> "Golf is a form of work made expensive enough for rich men to enjoy."—*Anon.*

> "I play golf in the 70s—when it gets colder, I quit."—*Anon.*

> "If you can smile when all around you have lost their heads— you must be the caddy."—*Anon.*

Emery Kelen, *American cartoonist, radio newscaster and writer, born Dec 22, 1896*
"An editor is a man who takes a French poodle, and clips him into the shape of a lion."

"Amendments are (a) The afterthoughts of law-makers, (b) A method of defeating a resolution by improvement."

"Lady Bird" (Claudia Alta Taylor) Johnson, *wife of 36th US President, born Dec 22, 1912*
"A politician ought to be born a foundling and remain a bachelor."

James C(laud) Wright, Jr., *American politician and Speaker of US House of Representatives, born Dec 22, 1922*
On the rhinoceros: "Here is an animal with a hide two feet thick and no apparent interest in politics. What a waste."

DECEMBER 23

Economists' Day
United States Federal Reserve System established Dec 23, 1913.

"If all economists were laid end to end—it wouldn't be a bad idea."—*Anon.*

"Inflation is like sin; every government denounces it and every government practises it."—*(Sir) Frederick (William) Leith-Ross, English diplomat and economist, born 1887 (birth date not available)*

"Political economy: two words that should be divorced on grounds of incompatibility."—*Anon.*

DECEMBER 24

Matthew Arnold, *English poet, essayist and literary critic, born Dec 24, 1822*
"One has often wondered whether upon the whole earth there is anything so unintelligent, so unapt to perceive how the world is really going, as an ordinary young Englishman of our upper class."

Michael Curtiz, *American director and actor, born Mihály Kertész, Dec 24, 1888*
"The next time I send a fool for something, I go myself."

Patrick Campbell, *English business executive and writer, born Dec 24, 1909*
"Journalism is the only job that requires no degrees, no diplomas and no specialised knowledge of any kind."

Christopher Andreae, *American financier, born Dec 24, 1919*
"Ignorance is a *right*! Education is eroding one of the few democratic freedoms remaining to us."

Ava Gardner, *American actress, born Lucy Johnson, Dec 24, 1922*
"After my screen test, the director clapped his hands gleefully and yelled: 'She can't talk! She can't act! She's sensational!' "

"I don't remember how many swimsuits I wore out—without getting near the water. I shot enough sultry looks around the MGM photo gallery to melt the North Pole."

DECEMBER 25

Joseph M. Schenck, *American pharmacist, director, producer and film executive, born Dec 25, 1878*
"We are not stalling, just procrastinating."

Humphrey (DeForest) Bogart, *American actor, born Dec 25, 1899*
"Bogey's a helluva nice guy until 11:30 PM. After that he thinks he's Bogart."—*Dave Chasen about Humphrey Bogart*

"The trouble with the world is that everybody in it is three drinks behind."

Quentin Crisp, *English actor, poet, writer and critic, born Denis Pratt, Dec 25, 1908*
"Vice is its own reward."

"The union of two hearts whose incomes are equal is a waste of time."

"If at first you don't succeed, failure may be your style."

"If one is not going to take the necessary precautions to avoid having parents one must undertake to bring them up."

"The trouble with children is that they are not returnable."

"Never keep up with the Joneses. Drag them down to your level. It's cheaper."

(Lord) Noel Gilroy Annan, *English army officer and university administrator, born Dec 25, 1916*
"Academic staff rather enjoy coming to a conclusion, but they don't like coming to decisions at all."

DECEMBER 26

Boxing Day in Canada, England, and Australia (observed on the following day when Dec 26 is a Sunday)

National Whiner's Day
"Man who beef too much find himself in stew."—*Anon.*

Helen Rowland, *American columnist and poet, born Dec 26, 1875*
"The hardest task of a girl's life is to prove to a man that his intentions are serious."

National Whiner's Day

"The follies which a man regrets most are those which he didn't commit when he had the opportunity."

Ed (Michael) Bluestone, *American physician, consultant, teacher, hospital administrator and editor, born Dec 26, 1891*
"If God wanted sex to be fun, He wouldn't have included children as punishment."

Henry (Valentine) Miller, *American novelist, born Dec 26, 1891*
"Everything that happened to me happened too late.... It was even so with my birth. Slated for Christmas, I was a half hour too late."

Alan King, *American comedian and producer, born Irwin Alan Kniberg, Dec 26, 1927*
"If you want to read about love and marriage you've got to buy two separate books."

DECEMBER 27

Louis Pasteur, *French chemist, born Dec 27, 1822*
"There are always people in whose presence it is unsuitable to be over-modest, they are only too pleased to take you at your word."

Marlene Dietrich, *German actress and singer, born Maria Magdalene von Losch, Dec 27, 1901*

"Latins are tenderly enthusiastic. In Brazil they throw flowers at you. In Argentina they throw themselves."

"I am not in the least disturbed when people regard my legs intently. I know they are doing so in pursuance of their inherent artistic instinct."

Oscar Levant, *American pianist, composer, actor and writer, born Dec 27, 1906*

"Oscar was a man of principle. He never sponged off anybody he didn't admire."—*Harpo Marx about Oscar Levant*

"There is absolutely nothing wrong with Oscar Levant that a miracle can't fix."—*Alexander Woollcott about Oscar Levant*

"Strip away the phony tinsel of Hollywood and you find the real tinsel underneath."

"I'm a controversial figure: my friends either dislike me or hate me."

"I've given up reading books. I find it takes my mind off myself."

"My behavior has been impeccable; I've been unconscious for the past six months."

"There are two sides to every question: my side and the wrong side."

"Underneath this flabby exterior is an enormous lack of character."

"I hate a sore winner."

"So little time and so little to do."

"What the world needs is more geniuses with humility, there are so few of us left."

DECEMBER 28

(Thomas) Woodrow Wilson, *American lawyer, educator, politician and 28th US President, born Dec 28, 1856*

"... while I was a lawyer, I have repented."

"Sam" (Samuel) Levenson, *American comedian and writer, born Dec 28, 1911*

"Insanity is hereditary. You can get it from your kids."

"Somewhere on this globe, every ten seconds, there is a woman giving birth to a child. She must be found and stopped."

"The reason grandparents and grandchildren get along so well is that they have a common enemy."

DECEMBER 29

Historians' Day

"Very few things happen at the right time and the rest do not happen at all. The conscientious historian will correct these defects."
—*Herodotus, Greek historian, born 5th century B.C.*

"The easiest way to change history is to become a historian."
—*Anon.*

"The memories of men are too frail a thread to hang history on."
—*John Still, English tea planter, archaeologist and writer, born 1880 (birth date not available)*

"History is something that never happened, written by a man who wasn't there."—*Anon.*

"The past is a work of art, free of irrelevancies and loose ends."
—*Max Beerbohm*

Janet Beresh, *American businesswoman, born Dec 29, 1942*
"The grass always looks greener on the other side [of the fence]; learn to live with yellow grass."

DECEMBER 30

(Joseph) Rudyard Kipling, *English poet and novelist, born Dec 30, 1865*

"If the aunt of the vicar
Has never touched liquor
Look out when she finds the champagne."

"A woman is only a woman, but a good cigar is a smoke."

"All the people like us are We,
And every one else is They."

Stephen (Butler) Leacock, *Canadian educator, economist, writer and humorist, born Dec 30, 1869*

"Advertising may be described as the science of arresting the human intelligence long enough to get money from it."

"Many a man in love with a dimple makes the mistake of marrying the whole girl."

"It takes a good deal of physical courage to ride a horse. This, however, I have. I get it at about forty cents a flask and take it as required."

DECEMBER 31

Make Up Your Mind Day

"Despite the millions spent on cosmetics research, no one has found a formula for making up your mind."—*Bruce Dexter*

"An evil mind is a constant solace."—*Anon.*

Elizabeth Arden, *American beautician and cosmetics manufacturer, born Florence Nightingale Graham, Dec 31, 1878*

"Nothing that costs only a dollar is worth having."

Index of People

Comment by Red Skelton at Louis B. Mayer's funeral.

† indicates the person is not quoted but his/her birthday is a holiday.
* indicates the person is not quoted but quote(s) and/or fact(s) about him/her are given.
Dates in italics are not birth dates
A listing by month only means the item appears in the text at the beginning of that month.

Index of Holidays

Note: A month without a specific date refers to material located at the beginning of that month.

Diets and Dieting

A listing by month only means the item appears in the text at the beginning of that month.